SUSSEX BY THE GLASS

Wines, vines and two pioneering families

SUSSEX
BY THE
GLASS

Wines, vines and
two pioneering
families

Liz Sagues

Liz Sagues (signature)

Dear Taylor
Good luck with your
new venture in vines!
Tamara.

Tanwood Press, Chichester

First published in 2021 by Tanwood Press, Chichester, West Sussex, 46/PO19 5RY

A CIP catalogue record for this book is available from the British Library.

ISBN 978-1-5272-8442-5

Designed by Liz Sagues
Cover design by CookChick Design Ltd, Brighton, East Sussex, BN1 4JZ www.cookchick.com
Printed by Selsey Press Ltd, Selsey, Chichester, West Sussex, PO20 0QH www.selseypress.co.uk

Front cover: left, Bolney vineyard (photo by Chris Orange, *www.chrisorange.com*), *right, Ridgeview vineyard* (photo Ridgeview Wine Estate)
Page 1, Pinot noir at Ridgeview (photo by XDB Photography)
Frontispiece: winter vines at Bolney (photo Bolney Wine Estate)
Opposite: the view from Ridgeview to the South Downs (photo by Sam Moore)

Contents

Introduction 7

1 How it all began 11

2 Progress, in so many ways 23

3 The wine year, month by month 41

4 Stages towards success 67

5 Will there ever be too much? 75

6 The future, still as well as sparkling 87

Pioneers: the family trees 93

Acknowledgements 94

Index 94-96

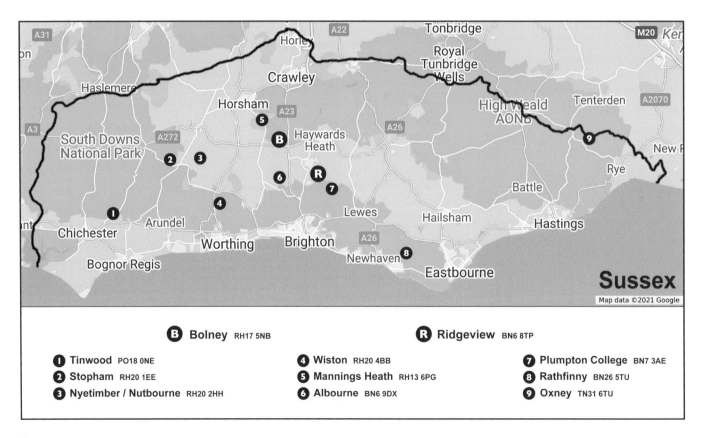

B **Bolney** RH17 5NB   **R** **Ridgeview** BN6 8TP

1 **Tinwood** PO18 0NE

2 **Stopham** RH20 1EE

3 **Nyetimber / Nutbourne** RH20 2HH

4 **Wiston** RH20 4BB

5 **Mannings Heath** RH13 6PG

6 **Albourne** BN6 9DX

7 **Plumpton College** BN7 3AE

8 **Rathfinny** BN26 5TU

9 **Oxney** TN31 6TU

Introduction

There's a lot of emphasis on English wine being something new. It is – and it isn't. Wine has been made here almost continuously through the 2,000 years since the Romans arrived. But the story of the wines that today are such a pleasure to drink, eyes shut, origin unknown, began little more than five decades back. That was when serious winemaking on a sizeable commercial scale was established alongside the hobbyist efforts, to be followed some twenty-five years later by the bubbling eruption of fine sparkling wine.

Yet too many wine drinkers still know next to nothing about the liquid that comes from vines planted through much of the south of England and beyond, far out to the east, west and north. Misconceptions abound – that English wine is unreasonably expensive, for example, or it's tooth-achingly acidic. Confounding them is one reason for this book. The aim is to tell a true and happy story, and to make it more relevant and personal by focusing on Sussex, the county that produces more English wine than any other, and on two respected wine estates within it.

Why Sussex? County boundaries are irrelevant to vines, but southern England – especially with a warming climate – is proving an increasingly good place for them. Soils, for one thing: the South and North Downs are a north-western continuation of the 100-million-year-old chalk of the Paris Basin, whose northern slopes are the home of champagne. English winemakers are often keen to stress how their vines have their roots in soils exactly the same as those that produce Krug or Cristal.

Between the Downs lies a swathe of greensand, an older marine deposit that can provide a warmer base and help grapes to ripen well. There's clay too. And there is a huge amount of discussion over which soils, which locations – low and sheltered, high and exposed – are best. What is most important is that today's vine growers are highly professional in every way, from choosing their planting sites to handling the ripe grapes they pick.

Twenty-first century weather in southern England is increasingly kind to grapes; long gone are the days when chardonnay berries looked, in the words of one expert, 'like frozen peas' as they were harvested. There will be more discussion of weather later, for the change is bad as well as good. But it has made grape ripening so much more consistent recently. And the longer, temperate growing season is giving

English growers an advantage over their colleagues across the Channel, where sometimes now summer is too hot.

All this is true of Kent and Hampshire as well as Sussex, and other counties as widespread as Essex and Gloucestershire, Cornwall and Yorkshire are showing great wine can be made in many, many English locations.

But Sussex is special. It is the home of Nyetimber, the wine that first put England into the world league of top sparkling wines. It is the location, too, of Plumpton College, whose Wine Division is a world-respected teaching and research resource. Plumpton graduates are making fine wines in England and beyond; in 2016 the college hosted delegates from 30 countries at the International Cool Climate Wine Symposium. And Sussex is the first wine region in England to be in line for its own PDO – protected designation of origin status.

Sussex is home as well to the Bolney and Ridgeview estates. Both are pioneers who have proved that English wine can be a sustainable business, a lot more than a retirement hobby or an indulgent second career for wealthy investors. Both are now in the hands of the second generation, which is a long time in an industry that started to take its modern form barely 50 years ago. They are, and have been for many years, in the forefront of showcasing what is currently Britain's fastest-growing agricultural sector.

Bolney Wine Estate, 50 years old in 2022, was one of the tiny group of commercial vineyards that laid the foundations for today's national success in both still and sparkling wine production. Ridgeview Wine Estate toasted its 25th birthday in 2020; it was the second of the two sparkling wine producers that established England as a rival to France, Sussex as a challenger to Champagne.

As a result, these two vineyards count as venerable producers of 'new' English wine. But they are important for more than that. Crucially, both were started and continue to be run by the same families. That may be only a brief record compared to the ancestral heritage some of their European counterparts can proudly record – but for England, even second-generation family vineyards that have proved to be long-term, successful businesses are rare creatures.

The estates are neighbours, eight miles apart. The people who run them are good friends and collaborators in the continuing tradition that has done so much to raise the quality of modern English wine. They are both headed by daughters of their founders, with brothers and husbands working alongside them. And both daughters have an influence beyond their own estates, beyond the Sussex boundary, through board membership of WineGB, the trade body overseeing their industry.

Yet Bolney and Ridgeview are different enough to illustrate

the increasingly broad story of English wine. One is tightly focused, putting its label on just seven bottle-fermented sparkling wines. The other has a much wider range, of still as well as sparkling wines with – for England – unusual emphasis on red grapes. Both recognise the importance of wine tourism and welcome visitors, but their offers are individual. Both make wine for other grape growers (there are far more vineyards than wineries in England, so that role is invaluable), but again they approach it in somewhat different ways.

What matters, too, as English (and Welsh) wine pushes to increase its sales and its popularity, is that Bolney and Ridgeview are names that consumers know. While both estates produce very fine wines for special occasions, they don't shy away from putting bottles on supermarket shelves. Those are where so much wine is sold these days, and English wine will achieve the success it deserves only if it has a prominent place on them alongside its world-wide companions, ready for all wine-browsing shoppers to pop into their trolleys.

Join me in raising a glass to the continuing success of both estates, and in thanks for their enthusiasm and support. Without that, this book would not have been possible.

Key in the success of modern English wine are graduates from Plumpton College. Photo, of Sally MacGarry, Plumpton College

Chapter 1

How it all began

In the story of modern English wine, a decade is a long time. After all, it is barely 70 years since the first limited, rarely palatable stirrings of wine making's resurgence in dreary post-war Britain. Until maybe 30 years ago none but the most patriotic dinner party hosts would have dared put a bottle of local produce in front of their guests. Even in the first years of the 21st century many of the biggest names around now were not even a flicker of ambition on their owners' horizons. How times have changed.

There is, though, a two-millennia-long history behind a product that has now gained world-wide renown. Before the Romans arrived, the picture is hazy. Their Belgic predecessors did like a beaker or two, but the liquid was probably not home-produced. Things changed after 43AD when the conquering army demanded vast supplies as part of its daily ration. Most wine for the Roman legionaries was no doubt imported, but archaeologists have uncovered a large agricultural site in

Planting at Bolney, 2008.

Northamptonshire where grape pollen was prolific and the pattern of planting holes exactly replicated that of known wine grape-growing practice in southern France. That site, the excavators believe, wasn't alone.

Christian monks took over after the Romans left, needing wine for meal-time consumption as well as for communion, and there are records in the 900s of Saxon kings granting vineyards to loyal abbeys. A century later the Normans' passion for agricultural detail shows in Domesday Book – vines are listed growing at 42 locations, though for some unknown reason not a single one of them is in the modern counties of Sussex and Hampshire, today two of England's prime vine regions.

The planting, picking, fermenting continued. Chaucer's pilgrims were wine drinkers (as was the poet himself, who received a gallon-a-day allowance from King Edward III), and monastic vine cultivation remained important until the 1536 Dissolution. Even then the taste for wine didn't go away, and some at least of the new noble owners of former monastic

Good wine or bad? What the drinkers said...

Over the centuries, opinions on English wine have been wildly contrary. 'Send ships forthwith to fetch some good French wine' was King John's instant reaction when he tasted the brew of the monks of Beaulieu in the early 13th century.

Some 400 years on, diarist John Evelyn was similarly unimpressed. In 1655 he dismissed the product of a vineyard near Blackheath as 'good for little'.

Yet his fellow recorder of 17th century events, Samuel Pepys, clearly had an altogether happier experience when with friends he drank a bottle of 1666 vintage from grapes grown at Walthamstow. Pepys' verdict: 'The whole company said they never drank better foreign wine in their lives.'

In the 1750s, things were also going well. 'My wine had a finer flavour than the best champaign [sic] I ever tasted,' declared a surprised and delighted Charles Hamilton, whose vines at Painshill Park, Surrey, included Burgundian varieties. And in 1897 wines from Wales were declared 'eminently honest and

King John
Samuel Pepys

wholesome' by London wine merchant Hatch Mansfield as it listed eight styles produced at Castell Coch, a vanity vineyard project for the immensely wealthy third Marquess of Bute.

Hang on a bit... perfection hadn't been achieved. 'The grapes are too small and too green,' remarked the narrator in a Pathé film of the harvest at Hambledon in Hampshire in 1971, adding that the juice squeezed out of the press 'does not look attractive at all'.

But then, in a 1997 blind tasting in Paris, the debut vintage of Sussex grower Nyetimber's blanc de blancs became the first of many English sparkling wines to beat their rivals world wide – champagne included – and a new era began.

'The cascading foam of bubbles danced and dallied on your tongue, teasing you to laugh and sing.' Who else but Oz Clarke, one of the most respected of tasters, could pen that description of what has become the biggest gift from Sussex – and England – to wine drinkers.

vineyards preserved both vines and winemaking expertise for their own benefit.

By the 17th century there are records of named growers. One was Lord Salisbury, who in 1611 planted the first batch of a total 30,000 vines he imported from France. Another, John Rose, gardener to King Charles II, wrote about his experience – in 1666 he published *The English Vineyard Vindicated*. That wasn't the only book on the subject: four years later Will Hughes' *The Compleat Vineyard* referred in its subtitle to the 'long practised' planting of vines in England.

English vine growing and wine making continued, through good periods and bad, until the outbreak of World War One.

Then, for the first time in almost 2,000 years, everything stalled. After World War Two, the revival came only slowly, with pioneering research work particularly at Raymond Barrington Brock's experimental vineyard in Surrey, where he planted 600 grape varieties. Some flourished, many didn't.

Alongside Brock, George Ordish and Edward Hyams both grew vines and, more importantly, through books and radio broadcasts spread the word about how wine grapes could flourish in England. And in 1952, at Hambledon in Hampshire, Major-General Sir Guy Salisbury-Jones was brave enough to try to prove that, planting the UK's first modern commercial vineyard.

Which brings us to the founding of the two vineyards that this book celebrates. If you expect to hear romantic tales of decades-long dreams and their joyful realisation, prepare to be disappointed.

Bolney – or Bookers as it was known until 2006 – was the first, established by Rodney and Janet Pratt in 1972. Rodney, a chemical engineer who was to continue his professional career in the rubber industry alongside his vine growing, describes how he had been on a placement at Gutenberg University in Mainz during his degree studies.

'We spent most of our six months in the vineyards of Louis Guntrum. He was the person who showed us all that there was a difference between Niersteiner Domtal, Liebfraumilch and Mateus rosé and real wine.'

Back home from Germany, Rodney Pratt couldn't contain his enthusiasm. 'I had this marvellous idea – let's go and find somewhere to live that's got a few acres of ground and we can plant a vineyard, and I shall retire at 45.' With Janet's support the first half of that ambition was achieved. Five decades on, part two hadn't proved as straightforward. 'I'm 78 and still working – something has gone wrong there,' Rodney said as the 50th anniversary approached.

The land the couple bought was on the outskirts of the village of Bolney, north west of Burgess Hill. It was a classic if run-down smallholding – there had been pigs, some chickens, cereals and vegetables.

Living accommodation was a tiny bungalow that the previous owners had failed to clean after breeding dogs there, leaving such a mess that Janet had to apply Jeyes Fluid throughout before daring to move in. The smell of disinfectant lingered for years, recalls their daughter Sam Linter, now managing director and head winemaker .

As well as planting vines, the Pratts continued to run the land as a smallholding, with Janet doing the majority of the work. Income from vegetable and fruit sales at Brighton markets, alongside Rodney's income – working initially for

Rodney and Janet Pratt in 1960.

Firestone and later running his own natural rubber commodity broking business – paid for the wine project. 'Every penny Dad earned and Mum made out of the smallholding they put back into planting more vines and having the wine made,' Sam says. 'It was very, very, very hand to mouth.'

Before the Bolney story continues, let's journey the eight miles south east to Fragbarrow Farm, looking out towards Ditchling Beacon, the highest point of East Sussex. Cereals grew there until the mid 1990s, when Mike and Chris Roberts came on the scene. Unlike the Pratts, they weren't starting their careers with a plan to grow vines, make wine and retire early. And they had money to invest – from the sale of the computer company that they had built during the late 1980s.

The couple wanted to do something new, but what? Chris Roberts confirms the indecision: 'When we sold the previous business we didn't know what we were going to do next. But there was an inkling about wine...'

Both Chris and daughter Tamara, now chief executive officer of Ridgeview Wine Estate, emphasise Mike's love of the Champagne region and its wines, and describe how he rewarded high-achieving staff with bottles and trips there. 'But he hadn't looked at it as a business,' Tamara adds.

He had, though, began to question why similar wine was not being made in England. And other factors helped turn thoughts into practice. One was the fortuitous co-incidence that his computer business had been located on an industrial estate in Burgess Hill where the wine company that was to grow into current industry giant Chapel Down then also operated. Mike Roberts was curious, conversations ensued.

'I think that may have sparked him to think about it a lot

more seriously. It whetted his appetite,' says Tamara. 'Likewise when he started the IT company I'm sure he had no massive desire to do that, it was just the right opportunity, right place, right time, in the right circumstances.'

Computers or wine: in each case, she believes her father 'was willing to take a risk, a well-educated, a well-thought-out risk'.

A similar trajectory, though a slower one

In the early 1980s, IT was a fledgling industry, and it changed dramatically in the decade during which the Roberts grew their business. There are, Tamara points out, clear similarities to the sparkling wine industry into which her parents moved. 'That started in a very cottage-industry way and is now very big and professionally run. It's a very similar sort of trajectory.' A slower one, she acknowledges, but then it takes a lot longer to make and mature a sparkling wine than to develop a computer program.

As Mike and Chris Roberts decided on the new direction their lives were to take, something extraordinary was happening in Sussex, something that would fundamentally affect the future of English wine and all the revival producers, existing and future. Nyetimber had arrived on the scene.

What is now the UK's major luxury sparkling wine brand

The Roberts family when Mike was presented with his MBE in 2011.

is the result of the unexpected achievement of two emigrés from Chicago, Stuart and Sandy Moss. When they decided to retire from their successful business careers and move to England, Sandy had a dream to establish a small vineyard.

They bought land, but not just any land – their choice was the magnificent Nyetimber estate close to Pulborough, noted in Domesday Book precisely 900 years before the Mosses arrived. Vines? That's a crazy idea, said the agricultural pundits. Plant apple trees.

No, retorted Nyetimber's new owners. Vines it would be, but not the germanic varieties preferred then by almost all of England's growers. From the outset, they were determined to produce fine sparkling wines, the bubbles created by second fermentation in bottle – exactly the way that champagne is made – and they were equally determined to use the same grape varieties that flourished in the somewhat warmer though geologically similar conditions across the Channel. So chardonnay, pinot noir and pinot meunier, the holy trinity of champagne vines, went into the greensand-based soil of their estate in 1988.

The rest is history... The first wines the Mosses released, their 1992 and 1993 vintages, won award after award in the late 1990s. And they persuaded even the most sceptical tasters to accept that England could make sparkling wines on a par with the best in the world. Those wines could not, however, be called champagne. That's a jealously protected name allowed to be used only for wines made in one specific area of northern France.

There had been other innovators...

The Mosses were not the only people, however, to produce bottle-fermented sparkling wines in England in the 20th century. Raymond Barrington Brock had trialled them in post-war Surrey, where he made wines as well as growing grapes. Back in Sussex, inland from Hastings, David and Linda Carr Taylor had produced a commercial quantity from their bumper 1983 harvest – but the grapes were reichensteiner. And certainly other producers were experimenting. But it took the Mosses' unswerving purpose to set in motion a movement that shows no sign of stopping for a long while yet.

They didn't do it on their own. They took the best possible advice, from England's expert in sparkling wine, Kit Lindlar, and from the winemaking grandson of the founder of a leading

The historic Nyetimber estate.

Who needed French skills? The English got there first

Here's something for the patriotic to celebrate: the English knew how to make bottle-fermented wine at least thirty years before champagne's legendary creator Dom Pérignon entreated: 'Come quickly, I am tasting the stars.'

In 1662, a scientifically-minded doctor from Gloucestershire by the name of Christopher Merret had explained to the Royal Society how to create bubbles in bottles of wine by adding sugar and molasses to set off a second fermentation. In happy recognition of that, Ridgeview labelled its early bottles Cuvée Merret. Sadly, the name hasn't stuck as a generic title for the elegant 21st century product.

Returning to 17th century inventiveness, there could have been a snag in sparkling wine making. Bubbles in bottles create a lot of pressure. Being able to carry into practice what Merret described had been possible only because of the creation, some three decades earlier, of bottles strong enough to survive that pressure.

Again, an Englishman was responsible, Sir Kenelm Digby. He was an intriguing character, active in areas as diverse as diplomacy and alchemy, philosophy and cookbook writing. The relevant activity here is his ownership of a glassworks with a very, very hot furnace. Out of it came exceptionally strong bottles, made from a mix including a lot more sand than usual in those days and even resembling modern sparkling wine bottles with their deeply indented base. No more explosions in the wine cellar...

Sir Kenelm Digby

champagne house, Jean-Manuel Jacquinot (both also worked with other vineyard owners, and are due much credit for the fine modern wines that are their legacy), and Sandy Moss studied at Plumpton College.

When Mike and Chris Roberts bought Fragbarrow Farm, they knew what might be possible, and they too decided to make top-quality sparkling wine in champagne style, from the champagne grape varieties. Mike went to Plumpton to study winemaking, and learnt French. He and Chris travelled to vineyards, talked to growers, winemakers, distributors. They also benefitted from the mentoring of Lindlar and Jacquinot.

But success was more complicated than they had anticipated. The money they thought would generously cover the project rapidly vanished out of the bank. 'Everything had to be hands on, we couldn't afford someone else to do it,' Chris recalls. That close personal involvement, though, fitted with their perfectionism. 'It was very exciting, but also very frustrating and very worrying; more money had to be spent.

We were determined that if we were going to do it we were going to make the best.'

The respect for Ridgeview, from the first wines to the continuing innovation today, confirms ambition achieved. More than that, the Roberts family developed their business in one immensely important way – it made Ridgeview the brand that introduced a broad spectrum of wine drinkers to the pleasures of English fizz.

Today, there is a stark difference between Ridgeview and Nyetimber that reflects broader changes in the English wine industry. 'The investment Nyetimber have had has catapulted them to a huge brand,' Tamara Roberts explains. 'We have had to grow in a much more organic way.'

The two companies are also set apart in another important way: while Nyetimber has passed through several hands, Ridgeview remains the original family's business. That, too, is the case with Bolney. How, in both, did the founders' children come on board?

The Pratts' business mix of wine, vegetables and rubber meant an unconventional life for middle-class children who might otherwise have gone to private schools and enjoyed

Janet and Rodney Pratt with daughter Sam as a baby, and Rodney selling the estate's wine.

holidays abroad. Sam and her brother Mark loved the freedom to roam the countryside, to ride – in the days when health and safety regulations were minimal – on the combine harvester in the field where chardonnay vines now flourish, to camp in the surrounding woods. 'We had a blast,' Sam recalls. But there were downsides: 'We lived in hand-me-down clothes, had no family holidays, no treats, we didn't have biscuits, cakes, desserts.'

No wonder she proved a rebellious teenager, hating school and refusing all entreaties to choose a college or university course. She ended up, almost accidentally, taking a hairdressing apprenticeship. Faced with an ultimatum from her parents that they'd choose a college course for her 'it was the first thing that came into my mind'. 'I can't say I ever enjoyed hairdressing – it's a very creative occupation, but it wasn't for me.'

She persevered for ten years, though for the last five she taught rather than trimmed. By then, the early 1990s, her father was an independent rubber trader working from home. He needed some admin help, so in 1995 Sam stepped in to work with him. Of course, she couldn't escape what was going on in the wine side of the business.

It was an opportune moment. Kit Lindlar, who had been making the wine, gave up contract work. Rodney Pratt and his brother-in-law took over, with a couple of existing tanks,

a cheap press and not very much expertise. 'It was quite amusing,' Sam says. 'They worked really hard at it with little knowledge of what they should be doing. So then I said, you know what, if we are going to do this one of us needs to know how to make wine. Why don't you send me to Plumpton and I'll learn to make wine and then we'll do it properly.' And that's what happened.

Rodney had confidence in his daughter, which she appreciates. 'In everything we have done here at Bolney when it came to the winemaking side he's really stood back and let me do it, which has been great.'

One silver lining to the dark clouds

But business-wise, what had been going on earlier wasn't great. The Pratts had found selling their wine hard – with one notable exception. Rodney recounts the surreal conversation he had with a Financial Times journalist in the mid 1970s. 'I was telling him about price of natural rubber, he wanted to know why I had planted grapes.' Confusion reigned until Rodney realised that the journalist's purpose was to learn more about the Pratts' müller-thurgau wine that, remarkably for the time, had just won a silver medal in the International Wine and Spirit Competition.

'We actually hadn't entered it – one of our customers had,

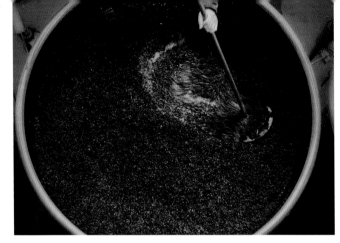

Red wine fermenting at Bolney.

because they thought it was terrific. So we sold that vintage out in two days. That success persuaded me to carry on.'

Subsequent vintages gathered dust, however. Before Sam could offer the results of her new skill to Bolney customers there was the small matter of 10 years' worth of wine sitting in the vineyard's bonded store. What to do with it? The bottles were sorted into those that were still good, and the rest disposed of. Selling the good was hard; it was still the time when the reputation of English wine remained poor: 'Nobody had any interest in it, nobody wanted to taste it, and those that were brave enough to taste it didn't like it anyway.'

She toured agricultural shows around Sussex and beyond. When visitors to her stand realised what she was offering the

reaction was an 'oh my goodness, English wine – you must be joking, it's really bad'.

Generally, they were right. 'It was very poor,' Sam acknowledges. 'There were some good wines, but it wasn't consistent.' That was down to a series of factors: the wrong choice of grape varieties, little knowledge of good vineyard practice and how to handle disease, a lack of investment.

'When my parents started in the 1970s nobody knew anything. Only a handful of commercial vineyards had been planted before then, and everybody was desperately learning. Nobody, actually, knew how to grow vines in England. They just didn't. So it was a massive learning curve.'

By the time Sam was back at Bolney – the year that, coincidentally, saw the establishment of Ridgeview – English wine producers had learned a lot, though there was much still to understand. 'I dread to think of all the money my parents spent and lost learning how to grow vines and the right grape varieties.'

They had, though, been brave investors. 'In the mid 1980s my parents planted 10 different grape varieties in a new field they managed to buy,' she continues. 'They knew they had to do something else.' They planted cool-climate varieties including the reds rondo and dornfelder – and also chardonnay and pinot noir. Slowly, the realisation came that the two French classics 'grew really well in the site we have here and we could do something more interesting with them'. That was the beginning of a period of experimentation. 'There were so many things going on. It was incredible.'

Sam Linter has continued the innovation. In 1998 she made Bolney's first red wine, a rondo-dornfelder blend. 'It was semi-decent, but we needed to do a whole lot better.'

Within a few years, she had. Something quite exceptional happened in 2007: Bolney secured the first-ever supermarket listing – in Waitrose – for an English red wine, the 2004 vintage of a blend very similar to that first example. Its successors are on the shelves as I write.

Fewer challenges, but still many risks

Ridgeview, with its specific focus on sparkling wine and classic champagne grapes, avoided many of the challenges faced by Bolney and the other early commercial vineyards. Even so, Mike and Chris Roberts were pioneers in something very new, stepping into the near-unknown with all the risks that entailed.

Initially, it was a project for them alone. Simon, their son, was in Cornwall, learning to build boats; daughter Tamara was studying to qualify as a chartered accountant, after completing a law degree.

With her parents' wine business at its very beginnings,

with no indication of whether or not it would succeed, Tamara was certain she should continue with an independent career, which took her to a senior role in a major finance company. 'I remember sitting and thinking: what on earth are they doing.' Would there be wines, would buyers like them?

Almost a decade later, there was no more room for doubt,

Tamara and Simon Roberts. Photo by Carol Sachs

even though Ridgeview wines had been on sale for only four years. Why had it taken so long for them to reach appreciative drinkers? All sparkling wine producers face this inevitable time-lag: vines must be allowed to grow for three years before the first proper harvest, then comes another three years for the wine to be made and matured.

'Relatively soon after we'd started selling, it became apparent that there was a future here,' Tamara explains. 'The family decision was that we wanted to grow the business and make it successful, so I came on board in 2004 as general manager working alongside Dad.'

By then Simon also was thoroughly involved, on the winemaking side. He had helped to plant the first vines and liked the hands-on side of the new business – it tempted him away from his first love, sailing, where he had intended his career to lie. 'He came in, just fell in love with it,' says his sister.

Simon had had no intention of staying at Ridgeview after those few weeks of planting, but 'by the end of that summer I realised I loved farming', he recalls. So off he went to learn viticulture at Plumpton.

The permanent change to winemaking came rather later, and unexpectedly – thanks to an experience in a German monastery. He recounts that he, his father and Kit Lindlar had gone on a trip to a winery equipment show at Stuttgart. En route, Kit took them to meet a friend who was winemaker in a monastic winery. 'I didn't speak German, I didn't really drink wine back then.'

Into the early hours, they tasted from vats and barrels, and Simon was occasionally asked his opinion. Afterwards, the winemaker confided to Mike and Kit: 'This boy has got a really good palate.' That decided Simon's move from vineyard to cellar. Shelf-loads of awards and trophies later, he continues to head the Ridgeview winery team.

Recognition of her brother's exceptional palate was just part of the myriad happenings as the business developed, Tamara continues. 'It was exciting – it was a new learning curve, a complete new language.

'We don't come from a wine background, no-one had worked in the wine trade. Sometimes that is quite refreshing, because you are coming at it without any baggage or preconceived ideas, maybe asking stupid questions. But then having the guts to ask the stupid questions can sometimes really help because people aren't expecting it. You start to ask: but why are we doing it like that, why, why, it doesn't make any sense…'

But it has.

Chapter 2

Progress, in so many ways

Now, English wine is loved by consumers, for its floral, hedgerow scents, its crisp and appealing fruit, its lack of over-the-top alcohol. The essence of summer, to be enjoyed all year round. Why, in the past, was it often so poor?

'One of the problems was that everyone planted müller-thurgau, which produced a rather indifferent wine.' In that verdict, Rodney Pratt is being generous. His daughter is less kind. It was 'a disaster' to plant that and many other germanic varieties, Sam Linter argues.

They didn't like English rain, there was pervasive mildew and rotten grapes, the German agricultural consultants whose help was sought offered the wrong advice for England's different climate, the inexperienced winemakers failed to realise that bad grapes made bad wine. 'Rightly, the wine had a very bad reputation,' she adds.

Of course, there were exceptions, especially as English winemakers learned to add a little sugar to balance the acidity of their 'mostly thin, lean whites' (that description is from

The mower doubles as tractor to pull a home-made trailer during harvest at Bolney in the late 1980s.

Oz Clarke – over the years he has probably commented, increasingly favourably, on more English wines than any other popular wine writer), and the germanic varieties began to be handled in a way that hinted at the pleasures so characteristic of English wine now.

Though progress was being made with still wines before the sparkling revolution, the years spanning the end of the 20th century and the start of the 21st were a crucial period for everyone involved in wine production in England.

The shadow cast over still wines as the sparklers attracted growing attention at home and abroad was, in retrospect, something of a benefit. It allowed still wine producers to make progress quietly in the background, continuing to select better grape varieties and rootstocks, to implement canopy management, to learn that they could ripen grapes properly – even red grapes – and to control acidity in the finished wines. The emphasis moved from quantity to quality.

But that focus on sparkling wines had a downside, too. Just as English still wines were improving very appreciably, they faded from mainstream attention. They have emerged from the shadows only slowly, which is a great shame for drinkers as well as for producers.

There are more and more good still wines now that can compete with renowned names in the wine world – and, to counter one regular argument, they are not over expensive.

Julia Trustram Eve, marketing director of industry trade body WineGB, argues that consumers need to compare UK still wines with, for example, styles such as sancerre or chablis rather than high-yield, low-cost warmer climate sauvignon blanc or chardonnay. And Sam Linter is insistent that producers must continue to put quality first, aiming for low yields and better ripeness.

Making any wine in England is far costlier than in many wine nations. Land and labour aren't cheap, yields are low and government tax regimes don't make exceptions for the home-grown product. There is economic sense in producing good still wines – the return on initial high investment comes at least two years sooner than it does with sparkling wines.

No outsiders were ready to invest

Which brings us neatly to the saying that has been doing the rounds for years: 'If you want to make a small fortune out of English wine you need a large fortune to start with.' Inevitably, money features in every discussion of past – and of present and future.

No outside investment was on offer for the pioneering post-World War Two English wine producers. Rodney Pratt recalls how very hard it was at the beginning: 'We didn't

Stopham Estate, near Pulborough: a Sussex specialist in still wines.

have money to do everything at once, we had to fund it out of income, which was difficult but we succeeded. Most of the equipment we had was second or third or fourth hand. I used to spend the weekends repairing it.'

Daughter Sam confirms the struggle: 'The money Dad earned went to buying another field, planting more vines, buying machinery. It went to everything really.'

Finally, the slowest of changes in investment attitudes began early in the 21st century. 'English wine had to prove itself,' Sam continues. 'It was really tough to take your business and the quality of wine you were making to a level that started gaining a reputation where you could borrow the money you needed to take it to the next level.'

European Union grants began to help around 2005, and encouraged English banks to part-fund, for example, new winery buildings – Bolney was one to benefit. But until much

more recently there was no help towards planting the vines themselves. Scarcity of investment put a block on progress, on innovation. 'It was all done little by little, slowly stepping up. We missed so many opportunities because our financial resources, over all those years, went to learning how to grow vines and grow grapes and make wines. My parents and the people around them, they really were the pioneers. They believed that it could be done, they invested every penny they had into proving their point and making it work.'

For the Roberts family at Ridgeview, despite the high profile of sparkling wine, the experience has been similar. 'Back when we started, and until very recently, options available for finance were very limited because the industry was just not understood, just not thought of as a proper industry worth investing in,' says CEO Tamara. She notes with relief one very recent opening, inventory finance – loans secured on wine

Models to follow: the champagne widows

Today's female wine students could look to role models earlier than Sam Linter or Tamara Roberts. Not simply within the UK wine trade or broader businesses, but very specifically – in champagne, so relevant to English wine producers today.

Barbe-Nicole Ponsardin, la Veuve Clicquot, is the best known of 19th and 20th century widows who controlled major champagne houses. But there were others: notably Louise Pommery, Mathilde Emilie Laurent-Perrier, Lily Bollinger, Apolline Henriot and Camille Olry-Roederer.

As widows, they had a freedom to be involved in business that had then been impossible for their unmarried or married sisters, who were excluded from financial independence. Between them, they left remarkable winemaking and commercial legacies.

Louise Pommery, for example, saw a new opportunity for champagne exports – to England, where she had been sent to boarding school. By the late 1860s, a middle-aged widow, she was heading the Pommery business and moving it from red wine to sparkling whites.

She knew that English drinkers preferred drier wines than the French, so she created the now immensely popular 'brut' style, with a much, much lower *dosage* (the final addition of sugar to sparkling wine, to soften its acidity), and saw her company's exports flourish. Almost 150 years on, Pommery was one of the first two champagne houses to buy vineyard land in England.

As the 19th century drew to its close, Mathilde Emilie Laurent-Perrier took that low-sugar innovation further, inventing a style that is starting to appear in English bottles – non dosage or ultra brut, where no sweetening at all is added.

After ensuring her company's champagne production continued during World War Two, Lily Bollinger was the third widow to add new styles to the market: champagne made from pinot noir grapes alone, and recently disgorged (RD). RD indicates a classic method wine that spends longer on its lees (the fermentation residue) and is disgorged and bottled just before drinking. The result combines the complex flavours of long ageing with freshness.

The most important legacy, and the broadest, predated all those. It was left by the first of the champagne widows, Barbe-Nicole Ponsardin, whose husband François Clicquot died in 1805. She was responsible for the invention of riddling, the regular turning of spar-

Barbe-Nicole Ponsardin

Louise Pommery

kling wine bottles after second fermentation so that dead yeast sediment ends up in the neck of the bottle, ready to be expelled before the wine is ready for sale. The house she ran also introduced vintage champagnes and the first rosés, made then as frequently they still are by adding a little red wine to the white base blend. Crucially, too, she ensured that Clicquot beat all rivals to regain the lucrative Russian market at the end of the Napoleonic wars. La Veuve Cliquot's contemporary, Apolline Henriot, was also an export innovator, with a different target: she focused on the royal courts of Europe and the Austro-Hungarian empire.

And bringing the story closest to today is Camille Olry-Roederer, who headed the house of Roederer for 43 years from 1932 and rebuilt its post-war fortunes. Sparkling role models indeed.

stocks. 'It's taken a long time and a lot of hard blood, sweat and tears from all us producers to get us to that position.'

Even when a wine estate is up and running well, financing is a minefield, she continues. 'This business is incredibly difficult for cash flow, it's capital intense, the big stock you've got sucks all your money out. You have to pay for all your production up front, your sales come along later.' When things go wrong – there's a poor harvest, or sales are delayed – it hurts.

An importance that stretches beyond wine

Their history and the quality of their wines apart, Bolney and Ridgeview are important in British business in a far broader way. For two leading companies in a new, admired and rapidly expanding industry to be headed by women is special, even in the 2020s. What is so encouraging is that Sam Linter and Tamara Roberts didn't get there because of any gender-equality intervention. Certainly, being family helped: they were in the right place at the right time. But they have proved they have the skills and ability to run and grow their businesses.

A professional background in high-level finance contributes to Tamara's confidence that she is 'completely competent' to be CEO of Ridgeview, a role she took on in 2014 after ten years as general manager. She has seen production grow from 25,000 to 400,000 bottles a year – a figure now with the potential to double following completion in 2020 of a new winery and cellar.

But there was a little help... 'I learnt an awful lot from my dad, I was very lucky to work so closely with him for so long. He was a brilliant man in terms of business and people and all sorts of other things.'

Often, she notes, there is a tendency to remark on the importance of women in wine, world wide, from heads of champagne houses to boutique winemakers. 'I think it's just brilliant now that it can be the daughter and it doesn't have to be the son. Before, there were loads of daughters who could do a much better job than their brothers but just weren't given the opportunity.'

Women do bring in something extra, she believes. 'I think there's a lot less ego, a lot less conflict. I think as a whole the females just want to get the job done. If things go wrong we don't tend to flap, we want to find out what's gone wrong and how do we fix it.' Perhaps, she adds, the blame culture is less. 'It's slightly calmer, maybe a little more forgiving.'

She regrets that even now women aren't sufficiently represented at board level in some leading wine trade organisations, and in business generally. 'Any company that doesn't have women on the board or in the senior management team is missing a massive trick, because balance is what it is all about. We just approach things in a different way. and that's really important.'

No longer so much a man's world
There was clearly a culture change in the decade between Sam Linter and Tamara Roberts joining their respective family businesses. 'When I first started in this industry, it was a man's world,' Sam remembers. 'There were very, very, very few females in there, and those that were in it had to fight very hard to be recognised. It wasn't easy.'

But she wasn't deterred: 'I grew up a little bit of a feminist, encouraged by my mother. She was a great lady. I was determined to not let anybody stop me from achieving what I wanted to achieve.' And she had experience of how to succeed, overcoming – with the firm support of her parents – her school's refusal to allow her to join what had been a boys-only woodwork class. 'So coming into this industry I was already used to having to stand up for myself against massive sexism.'

She instances what could happen, when, for example, she

had to buy tractor spares. There was always a delay while any male customers were served, a rudeness from the staff, a 'why are you here?' atmosphere. 'You really had to be very forceful, very pushy.'

When she first studied at Plumpton, in the late 1990s, she was the only woman on her course, and there were only two women winemakers in England. 'That has changed a lot in the last few years. There are a huge number of women involved now.' As Plumpton's courses expanded, both female and male students often came to Bolney and Sam would be regarded as their role model. That continues now. Similarly at Ridgeview, a long supporter of the college, students on work placements can be inspired by family and female leadership.

'We stick together'

Is there a sisterhood among women in English wine? That question prompts somewhat different responses. 'I'm really keen on building this,' says Tamara. 'When I started, I was quite surprised just how women were not particularly collaborative together or could be a little bit stand-offish. But I'd say that across the board in the last five years, maybe more, this has changed dramatically and women are really

Sam Linter (left) and Tamara Roberts (photo by Andrew Hasson).

looking out for each other, giving each other a lot of support.'

'I think it's more that we are very collegiate in the wine industry, there's a lot of us who work together,' says Sam. 'I wouldn't say there's a sisterhood as such, but I do agree women are looking out for each other. I don't think it should be about whether it's about females or about males, it's actually about the industry now. We stick together.'

There is, however, valuable contact between the women in English wine. 'We get together whenever we can,' says Tamara. 'We're all in the same industry, we're all like-minded. We're competitors, but we're all people at the end of the day.'

Across Sussex, other women-led estates include Albourne, to the west of Ridgeview and also facing the scarp of the South

Shepherd's hut with view of the vines: a place to stay at Oxney Organic Estate.

Downs. There, Alison Nightingale changed career from multi-national marketing to winemaking – and carried off the 2015 English Wine of the Year award for the first vintage of her bacchus still wine. She has continued that early success with newer vintages of her still wines, single varieties as well as blends, and fine sparklers.

On the eastern edge of the county, inland from Rye, Norwegian-born Kristin Syltevik dug in – literally – in 2012, planting many of the first vines on her Oxney Estate by hand, to create what has become England's largest single-site organic vineyard. Her new role is very different from her previous work in top-end public relations, and she revels in it, releasing much-admired still and sparkling wines. Additionally, she has developed the estate's wine tourism appeal, with holiday cottages and shepherds' huts, emphasising green credentials.

Oxney's visitor attractions are small scale compared to the ambitions of Penny Streeter, who has brought her South African 'golf and wine estate' concept to Mannings Heath, near Horsham, where the first grapes – intended for classic sparkling wine – were harvested in 2020. The vines replace nine holes of one of two previous 18-hole courses.

She also owns nearby Grade I-listed Leonardslee Gardens, which she restored to former glory, reopening them to the public in 2019 and incorporating a smart restaurant that rapidly gained a Michelin star. A year earlier, Leonardslee was the site of an experimental planting of pinotage vines. If Sussex summers don't ripen their fruit enough to make a still red the grapes likely to be turned into sparkling wine (as they are sometimes in South Africa).

A similarly strong-minded woman has brought a South African connection to another Sussex estate, Wiston, at Washington. But Pip Goring – whose French Huguenot ancestors

had established a vineyard in Franschoek – took 34 years to persuade her husband to convert a small part of the historic family estate to vines. She was right, as the sparkling results (made by Dermot Sugrue in the modern winery, converted from a turkey shed) are further example of highly regarded English wine.

And there is Nyetimber. Cherie Spriggs has been head winemaker, with her husband Brad Greatrix working alongside her, since shortly after current owner, Dutch-born lawyer and entrepreneur Eric Heerema, bought the estate in 2006. Perhaps, Nyetimber will in time become one of the Sussex multi-generation wine businesses. Cherie knows that her boss isn't in the business short term: 'He doesn't think in years, he thinks in generations.' Her role is to ensure that Nyetimber's wines always progress, not rest on their reputation.

It is crucial, Tamara Roberts believes, that women continue to hold major roles at Sussex estates, and in English wine generally. 'Having women at the top means you can actually carve the changes that are necessary within the business structure, to make it female friendly, family friendly, to create an environment in which people can balance the pressures of

Penny Streeter plants pinotage vines at Leonardslee,
with cellar master Johann Fourie.

home and work life.' With such flexibility, she argues, 'women actually give a lot more'.

Simon Roberts agrees. Barriers in what was previously a very male-oriented industry are, he argues, 'being very quickly broken down'. He believes the importance of women also helps reduce snobbery in the English wine industry. 'And that's something we have always been really proud of at Ridgeview, that we are really accessible, there isn't that snobbery or pretentiousness, you can pop into the winery or the shop and often one of the family will be around.'

At the end, it comes down to what is best for the business. 'As a family business me and my brother are involved and neither of us is more important than the other,' Tamara adds. 'That's the way it should be. We just have very different roles.'

The generation game

But whoever is at the head, female or male, can a family business always run smoothly? Surely there are times when generations clash, when there are very different views on what should happen. Sam Linter diplomatically points to an 'interesting dynamic' as Bolney moved forward. She understood her father's patriarchal attitude, even though it made life difficult at times.

'He was still working with his other business and he wasn't fully involved in the wine business. Things were changing when he wasn't really there to see it and I think he found that difficult because he still wanted to be in charge, wanted to make the decisions.

'Had we all known then what we know now we would have looked at how we worked as a family and how we ran the business and who was doing what. We would have said, these are the boundaries, these are the guidelines, this is the business plan, this is what we want to achieve. We didn't do that. There was no setting of boundaries, it was more a question of evolution.' But had she given up, she believes Bolney Wine Estate would not have survived.

Rodney Pratt

Since 2016 Rodney Pratt has partly retired – becoming president of the company – and talking to him it is clear how hard it has been to let go, despite his clear faith in Sam and the path she is taking.

Surely Ridgeview's saddest moment came on November 14th 2014, when Mike Roberts died. He was much more than the owner of a pioneering sparkling wine business. He was an inspiration and a mentor, a man who had immense influence in creating the much-admired industry that English sparkling wine is today.

'Mike was always very altruistic,' says his daughter. 'He would never turn anyone down.' Always, she continues, he was able to look beyond his own estate's horizon, to see a bigger picture. He could recognise that something perhaps not quite right for Ridgeview might be best overall, or that something the estate was doing right should be shared 'because it's going to be good for the whole industry'.

Mike Roberts

There was always help for newcomers

From very early on, Ridgeview helped newer followers, with planting, winery planning, winemaking. 'That was all around the fact that if we made sure the first wines that they made were really good wines then it was going to help the industry,' Tamara explains. 'The fact that they may go on to make their own brand and become competitors is a price we have to pay, but we've helped establish a quality level, a base against which all English sparkling wine will be assessed. And if that quality level is high then everyone else has to keep pushing the boundaries.' She defines the process as 'co-opetition': 'Being co-operative, a rising tide takes all.'

That help for others and its reflection within the whole English sparkling wine industry continues today, Simon Roberts notes: 'Without sounding arrogant, if Ridgeview is on board with something then people will think that's a good thing to follow. People will come to us and ask what have we done. You go to a lot of wineries now and it looks a little bit like another Ridgeview winery, which is a compliment.'

But there was a cost to Mike Roberts' commitment. 'He was a workaholic, and I think that is what finished him off. It was very hard to pull him out of work,' says Tamara. And sometimes there was a downside: 'There were definitely two sides to him. Fortunately the negative one was rare. He wasn't a massively social man, it wouldn't be his thing to do networking but he did well when he had to. He was human, he wasn't superhuman. He was good at getting it right 90 per cent of the time.'

Graham Linter with Sam, and children Matt and Charlotte in 1999.

There were strains, and the family bore the brunt of them. 'You do have much higher expectations of your family, expectations of effort, commitment, than you would of someone you were employing and that's not necessarily fair all the time because everyone has a life as well. That can sometimes be an area of tension you have to be aware as you grow as a family business.'

During that growth, she continues, there is a need to recognise that employees can't be expected to put in the same enormous effort – their lives outside the business matter. Now, there are thirty-plus members of the Ridgeview team.

The women who run Bolney and Ridgeview emphasise how much they value the support of their husbands – who both work in the businesses. Graham Linter's title is Senior Manager IT, but his role is very much more than overseeing everything computerised, which includes developing internal systems to link with software packages Bolney uses.

The list of jobs runs from maintaining weather stations to data protection regulation compliance, from general repairs when the maintenance man isn't around to 'making tea for the MD'. He has no fears of running out of work: 'It's obvious that digital is the future.'

He worked in finance and IT before Bolney, though he'd visit the vineyard with Sam, even helping to milk the goats her parents kept. The estate was 'a pretty special location' for their wedding reception. 'But generally in those days the whole idea of trying to make wine in England seemed totally daft to me!'

That view altered only slowly, even when Sam took over the winemaking. But changes where he worked prompted a decision to go self employed, and combine an outside project with taking over Bolney's bookkeeping – for the vineyard and also for the businesses of Rodney Pratt and his brother – then very reluctantly done by Sam's mother.

'So that's how I ended up working for the company, and I'm still here fifteen years later, albeit in a very different role.'

There's another family man at Bolney, Sam's brother Mark Pratt. He has two vineyards of his own, which adjoin the estate and are managed by it for him, and he generally lends a helping hand, particularly when machinery needs to be fixed.

Another marquee, more celebrations

Tamara Roberts and Simon Larder – 'Lardy' – had been friends since sixth form, and married in 1998, also celebrating in a marquee at the vineyard. Lardy's previous work, too, was unrelated to wine – in procurement at first in London and later with Sussex Police. He'd visited Ridgeview often, occasionally helping in the vineyard: 'It was always a very easy and friendly household.'

Three generations at Ridgeview, including Lardy (back left) next to Chris Roberts and her four grandsons.
Photo by Carol Sachs

Mardi Roberts. Photo by Julia Claxton

He and Tamara hadn't planned to work together. Then Tamara became Ridgeview's general manager, and made him the offer of two part-time jobs subsumed into one full-time one, focusing on food safety standards – essential for a wine business beginning to supply supermarkets. Of course, what he did has expanded.

He sums up his 'very non-sexy' role now as background management of all the tasks 'that allow other people to get on with other jobs' – aspects such as building infrastructure, health and safety, keeping contractors happy, and much, much more. 'I love it!'

The estate's communication director, his sister-in-law Mardi Roberts, says quite simply that Lardy is 'the glue' that holds Ridgeview together, 'making things happen'. Both have huge respect for Mike Roberts, and for Tamara. Lardy recounts how, when he told Mike he and Tamara wanted to marry, there was a single demand: not to step in the way of his future wife's career ambitions. 'He was a very driven man, and you can see that in his daughter.'

Chris Roberts has also moved away from the limelight. She has seen Ridgeview grow from its very hands-on beginning to something much bigger, more like the company whose sale made the wine initiative possible. That experience makes her invaluable in standing in for others, for example when coronavirus furloughing confined team members to homes away from the estate.

'And I'm quite good at repairing things...'

The co-operative, everyone-involved feeling was patent whenever I talked to the family. Mardi Roberts gives that an antipodean accent. She's very firmly from a wine background, but in Australia. She met Simon there – on the first day for both of them at innovatory wine producer Brown Brothers, where he was on work experience and she had a temporary job.

Her uncles were in the wine business, she had spent school and university holidays among the vines and, debating her future after finishing a law degree, working a vintage seemed a useful interim solution.

'I remember when Simon said his parents had a vineyard I was a bit stunned.' She knew nothing of English sparkling wine, though she realised 'it made sense on paper: I was really, really intrigued'. Travelling was her next object, so why not England? 'I fell in love with Simon, and with the brand.'

Then, 1999, Ridgeview was just four people, Mike, Chris, Simon and Mardi. Over the years there have been endless new challenges. 'If it had been the same job I don't think I would have been here now,' Mardi emphasises. 'It is wonderful to see how it has developed.'

Her role means she's a link between winery, vineyard and office, involved in all that goes on and thus perfectly placed to spread the word about the family company and also all that Sussex vineyards offer – she is involved in a number of organisations promoting the wines of southern England.

Next, the third generation

Two generations in English family wine businesses is still comparatively rare. Three is exceptional. At Bolney, Sam's daughter Charlotte is involved, managing tours and events as part of the hospitality team. But it wasn't what she had originally planned.

As a child, having grandparents who owned a vineyard seemed totally normal, and a winemaking mother 'was just what she did'. The estate was always the subject of family discussions, and she couldn't escape its dominating presence. 'I started to develop a love-hate relationship with the family firm. It was something I was always proud of, but it had a habit of taking over our lives and you can end up resenting that.'

No, she wouldn't become part of it, instead studying English with plans to become a teacher or writer. 'I was concerned I would never prove myself if I did not go my own way.'

So what changed her mind? 'In the end it was hard not to get drawn in. Everyone in our family (even those who don't work here) has a massive emotional investment in the business. It's a big part of our lives and we are very proud of it. I've been working here for many years now and still love it – I can't really imagine my life without Bolney being a big part of it, so I will stay and support it for as long as I am needed.'

That could be a long time, and it just might lead to a pivotal role. A lot of learning about the production side would be needed first: 'Even if I was not directly involved in production it's important to fully understand the process and to be able to work closely with our expert winemakers. If I did get the chance to run this business one day and follow in my mother's footsteps that would be living the dream, but it's impossible to say what will happen in the future.'

The route might not be easy. 'It is unusual to be a third generation family member in this industry and because of that it is hard to access support or to always understand how my role should develop. I'd love more of the third generation to show an interest in the future – or even the fourth.'

At Ridgeview, generation three is still at school. There are four boys, two from each of the second generation couples. Their career intentions change from week to week. 'They're more interested in the business than they have been in the past,' says Tamara. 'They've started to do bits and pieces, they're involved when we have events.'

But there won't be any pressure on them to be involved as they grow older and make definite decisions, she insists. 'I'd be delighted if any of them are interested and enjoy the whole ambiance and are dedicated like we are to it. This is a business you have got to love – a vocation really. It can be pretty tough. If they found joy in it, then absolutely it would be amazing.' Her sentiments are firmly echoed by the rest of the family.

At both Ridgeview and Bolney there is much for the latest generation to live up to. Tamara Roberts' business skill has been recognised in Sussex and beyond. In 2019 she was named Business Person of the Year in the Sussex Business Awards,

and was appointed president for 2020 of the International Wine and Spirit Competition as it celebrated the 50th birthday of its awards. It was the first time an English wine producer had been chosen. The distinguished list she joined is predominantly male, but includes such notable women in wine as Baroness Philippine de Rothschild and, also from Bordeaux, May de Lencquesaing of Château Pichon Longueville.

Tamara says she was 'hugely honoured' to take on the presidency, and saw it as an opportunity both to highlight the work of women in the wine industry and to raise the profile of English wine – 'the opportunities, the threats, the future, and where I feel our industry is going to move to – and bring in some of the global issues surrounding the world of wine in terms of sustainability and climate change'.

Opposite, Chris, Simon and Tamara Roberts with Ridgeview's award haul from the 2018 IWSC; right, Sam Linter receives the Sussex Business Women Excellence award in 2017.

The presidency follows the IWSC's decision in 2018 to declare Ridgeview its Winemaker of the Year – again a first for England in the competition, and acknowledgement in particular of Simon Roberts' talent.

More recognition arrived from the trade magazine Drinks Retailing News, where Tamara was placed 33rd in its 2019 list of the 100 most influential, authoritative and dynamic personalities in the UK wine trade. And a remarkable year concluded with Ridgeview becoming the first English vineyard to be included in the World's Best Vineyards top-50 list.

Many awards have been placed in Sam Linter's hands, too. In 2012 Bolney won its first IWSC gold outstanding medal and the competition judges named Sam the UK Wine Producer of the Year. Five years later came the inaugural UK Wine Awards (now renamed the WineGB Awards), a more rigorous, judged-to-international-standard replacement for the previous English and Welsh Wine of the Year Competition. What was widely considered to be the biggest accolade went to Bolney: it was named Winery of the Year.

And broader aspects of the estate were recognised in following years: also in 2017 Bolney was Medium Business of the Year in the Sussex Business Women Excellence Awards, and in 2020 it carried off the Spirit of Family Business Award from Family Business United, which celebrates and supports initiatives worldwide. Sam and her team were praised as 'passionate, pioneering, with a strong commitment to support the local community'.

Beyond running their own businesses, both Sam Linter and Tamara Roberts are helping to shape the broader English wine industry. Sam became involved in the South East Vineyards Association in 1997, initially as secretary. She took the chair in 2000, which gave her a place on the UK Vineyards Association board.

Tamara was one of the inaugural directors of WineGB – the national organisation for grape growers and winemakers that in 2017 united the UKVA and English Wine Producers – where two years later she was joined by Sam. They've had their work cut out, as female voices on a male-dominated board.

Ridgeview in January

Chapter 3

The wine year, month by month

There is an annual pattern to the wine year, with peaks and troughs of activity. Some tasks must be carried out at particular times, others are more flexible. Some are obvious, such as harvesting or bottling new wine. Others may need more explanation: the technique to rid sparkling bottles of sediment, for example, or the planning before new vines are planted. This chapter explains what happens month by month, outside and in.

As you read on, you'll find by far the longest sections are about what happens in the vineyard. That's logical, for talk to any accomplished winemaker these days and you'll be told that quality wine is made in the vineyard rather than in the winery: the less intervention there, the better the result.

January
Outside: time for a trim
As with all perennial plants that need an annual haircut – or something a bit more drastic – vines must be pruned when

Pruning at Bolney

Pruning practices

A raft of shapes is seen in vineyards throughout the world, from the low-growing bush vines found most often in southern France, Italy or Spain to the high pergolas used to keep grapes away from damp ground that are favoured in places such as northern Portugal – such pergolas were once common in England for energetic germanic varieties. There are even vines trained into a basket shape within a hollow in the soil in such very windy places as the Greek islands, or grown up trees – after all, the vine is naturally a climber.

Now, English vineyards largely follow one of the world's most popular training systems: single or double guyot, named after 19th century French viticulturist Jules Guyot. This bends one or two canes (as main vine stems are known) from each vine trunk along horizontal wires, each cane cut to leave a chosen number of buds from which the fruiting branches shoot up. A two-bud spur is left at the base of each cane to provide the new cane or canes for the following year. Sometimes, an extra main cane is left, a sacrificial precaution in case frost hits.

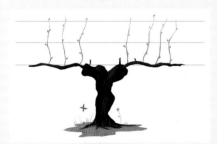

Double guyot pruning, with two horizontal canes from which the fruiting shoots grow up. Illustration by Anne Wilson, www.anne-wilson.co.uk

dormant, so this starts in November or December and continues through into February. There is much more to it than a simple tidy-up.

How the old wood is cut sets the pattern for the new growth and can make or break the next harvest. Do it right, and there are fewer but bigger and better bunches of grapes, rather than a glut of fruit that will never ripen properly. Fruit apart, controlling the future stem and leaf growth by judicious pruning begins the fight against disease. And the vines end up neatly ordered, allowing easier work around them through the rest of the year.

In some nations' large vineyard areas, mechanical pruning is practised. But English vines thrive thanks to skilled hand pruning (there are electric secateurs, to ease the effort – though to avoid the occasional digit being left among the discarded canes they must be used with extreme care).

Who wields the secateurs depends. In small vineyards, a live-in owner with perhaps a helper or two will do the work; larger growers will have their own part-time or full-time staff, or will use contract workers, often from Eastern Europe – Brexit created uncertainties here.

At Ridgeview, pruning is done by vineyard manager Matt Strugnell, his full-time assistant and some part-time workers, but the labour-heavy job of removing the cut branches from the trellises goes to specialist vineyard contractors Vine-Works. At Bolney the vineyard team aim to complete all the work themselves.

Inside: stability matters

In January, the latest vintage of still wines is nearing its final stages. Before bottling, wines need to be stabilised, to ensure what is later poured into the glass is clear and doesn't go off from bacterial contamination. The main wine antimicrobial agent is sulphur dioxide, which occurs naturally, but a little more is added, usually at bottling, for safety.

Already, racking to remove large unwanted particles has been done *(see November)*, but most winemakers will do more, to still whites and rosés especially. Cold stabilisation cools the wine down to -5°C to -10°C to precipitate out naturally occurring tartaric acid crystals, which look rather like tiny shards of broken glass. They're harmless, but off-putting if found in a bottle. Filtering, through a sterile powder or membrane, removes them and any other small solids.

Other contaminants are taken out by fining, a procedure that clogs them together for easy removal. Fining agents can be of animal origin (egg white, milk, fish bladders – none of these is used at Bolney or Ridgeview) or, increasingly, vegetable (pea or potato protein) or powdered minerals such as bentonite,

Cold stabilisation underway at Bolney, with Mike Hayward, production manager and assistant winemaker.

a type of clay. The enthusiasm for vegan or vegetarian diets and concern over allergies has spread into wine – for example, coopers no longer seal tiny cracks in barrels with flour and water paste, to ensure that no gluten escapes into the wine.

A further process, sparging, removes damaging oxygen. Fine bubbles of inert gas – nitrogen and carbon dioxide usually

Filtering at Bolney.

– are passed through the wine, pushing the oxygen out or dissolving it away.

Once all this is done, the wine is ready for blending – which is likely to be already underway this month – and bottling.

February
Outside: what happens to the prunings
Pruning continues – it needs to be completed by the end of the month. Bolney's mower/mulcher now passes through the vines, turning the pulled-out cut canes into a mulch, which improves the soil and helps to open it up. Other vineyards'

prunings and any dead vines should by now have been cleared away (good barbecue fuel for the summer...)

Inside: vintage or non-vintage
The pre-bottling processes for still wines continue, as does blending. For sparkling wines, blending is an essential part of establishing a 'house style', particularly for non-vintage wines where consistency year on year is the aim.

Depending on the potential components available – base wines from different grape varieties, vineyards, plots – and the palate of the blender, scores of individual base wines may be incorporated into what will become a single sparkling cuvée.

In England, until comparatively recently most classic method sparkling wines carried a vintage date: there simply wasn't the necessary stock of older wines to blend in, essential for consistency. Now many producers have them, so more non-vintage wines are available, with vintage wines often becoming the very carefully crafted top cuvées.

To celebrate Ridgeview's 25th birthday in 2020, Simon Roberts created a brand new style of wine for the estate, the limited-release Oak Reserve. That's a masterpiece of blending, with component base wines being matured in three-year-old barrels from Burgundy and five-year-old ones from the Loire Valley, as well as in stainless steel tanks.

March
Outside: tying down to encourage shooting up

This is the moment to set the pattern for the new season's growth. The canes are tied down to the lowest wire of the trellis, ready to encourage the fruiting shoots to grow upwards. Any remaining repairs to the trellis – the wires supporting the vines – are finished, and posts replaced if necessary. Also, soil preparation for the coming growing season needs to get underway. What's done at ground level, and later on the vines, depends on the philosophy of the vineyard owner.

Neither Ridgeview nor Bolney has gone down the organic route. Both respect those who do, but doubt its viability for their businesses.

They have, however, seen a dramatic reduction in the use of powerful, complex chemical treatments in their vineyards. Increasing limits on agricultural chemicals are reducing the choice available, but with sustainability high on everyone's agenda they anticipate more natural products becoming available to replace them.

Both producers use herbicides to keep the soil immediately under the vines clear, usually with a single treatment in March or April, followed later by mechanical weeding. Ridgeview has a particular difficulty with this, due to a layer of woven plastic through which the vines were originally planted. It

Green grass and clean grapes at Oxney Organic Estate.

Green grows my vineyard

Despite many naysayers, organic vine-growing can be successful in Sussex, as Kristin Syltevik has proved at award-winning Oxney Organic Estate in the east of the county, near Rye. Grasses and native plants have been allowed to establish themselves between the rows of vines, and grass and weeds around the vine trunks are lightly scratched away by a mechanical tiller set on the side of a tractor. Manure from animals grazing elsewhere on the estate and BSI certified compost are used to improve soil structure and encourage microbial life.

Inevitably, spraying is necessary against diseases, but with green-approved products alone. Against powdery mildew, Kristin uses sulphur and potassium bicarbonate, and a minimal amount of copper – well below levels permitted by the Soil Association – counters downy mildew. To treat botrytis she chooses a fungicide created from beneficial bacteria and approved for organic farming.

'Being organic isn't a tick list or a sales/marketing strategy – it is a state of mind and has to encompass everything you do,' she says, recounting how the previous evening she had watched a barn owl swoop by as she left the winery. 'There is a lot to eat in our vineyard, with long margins, lots of hedges and wild corners.'

was intended to restrict weed growth, but prevents any tilling. Removal began in the winter of 2020-2021.

As well, both are among the increasing number of estates where cover crops of meadow flowers and grasses are sown between the rows of vines, helping to encourage pest-attacking insects such as hover-flies and parasitic wasps. In winter, sheep graze in Bolney's vineyards.

Inside: corks or screw caps

The still wines of latest vintage are now ready to be bottled. Winemakers are often inordinately proud of their bottling lines, noisy machines that grab empty bottles, sterilise them, pour wine into them and seal them. Sometimes the same machine will also label the bottles, put on the foil caps, even pack them into boxes. They are very impressive, though once you've seen one...

But look carefully as the finished bottles come off the line. Are they sealed with a conventional cork, or is there a screw cap?

Back towards the end of the 20th century, there was a big problem with corks: an unpleasant compound called TCA (2,4,6-trichloranisole, resulting from the interaction of plant phenols, chlorine and mould) that spread from them into the wine, dumbing its scents and flavours and, in badly affected

Bud burst at Bolney.

bottles, ruining the liquid inside. That was 'corked' wine.

Examples are still around, but they are far, far fewer, thanks to the cork manufacturers cleaning up their act in a big way. TCA, however, was one reason why many wine companies – in Australasia initially – began using screw caps. Under them, the wine develops far more slowly in than in bottles closed with corks, and they're ideal for white wines best drunk young and fresh. But they aren't perfect. If winemakers overdo their efforts to reduce risk of oxidation, reduction results and the wine smells nasty when the cap is unscrewed.

Screw caps aren't of interest to producers of sparkling wine. In their wineries, as temperatures start to rise, it's time for *tirage*. Bottles are filled with blended base wine plus a mix of yeast and sugar, crown caps are crimped on and they're left on their sides for the bubbles to build – the secondary fermentation in bottle that creates champagne and every other classic method sparkling wine.

April
Outside: the buds begin to break

By now, unless spring is very late, the tight vine buds will be starting to open, sending out delicate pink-tinged pale green leaves enclosing the embryonic flower buds. They're very vulnerable to frost. If temperatures drop below freezing, all those new green shoots could be destroyed. If that happens and the growers are to have any crop at all, the secondary buds need to develop, but they will never compensate fully.

Much can be done to avoid frost damage. Weather forecasts are minutely monitored, and many Sussex vineyards have climate sensors installed, linked to the phones of designated staff members. When a warning goes off, it's full speed to the vineyard.

Commonest action there is to light *bougies*, large cans filled with paraffin or vegetable wax, to create a current of warm air rising among the vines. That's labour intensive, as these candles need to be extinguished once the day warms up.

Vineyards with more money to spend can invest in a variety of fans, the biggest capable of stirring up the cold air,

and thus avoiding it settling on the vine shoots, over an area as broad as five or six hectares. The tractor-driven frost-busters at Gusbourne Estate, which has vineyards in Sussex and Kent, are described as 'giant hair-driers'. They suck in cold air, warm it and push it out again.

Bolney uses a frost drain in its more vulnerable vineyards, a huge fan pulling out ground-level air and allowing warm air higher up to drop down and keep the temperature above freezing. It has to run constantly, until the frost risk is over, and vineyard staff have to leave their warm beds in the early

Bougies lit against frost at Ridgeview. Photo by Julia Claxton

The UK's most popular present-day grapes: the champagne trilogy

April and May are the months for expanding or replanting vineyards. Two grape varieties stand way above the rest in popularity now. Almost 60 per cent of new plantings are of chardonnay and pinot noir, in roughly equal shares, and the third of the champagne trilogy, pinot meunier, comes next, at just above 10 per cent. The vast majority of these new vines are intended for sparkling wine, though still wines are also made from them. Varieties destined largely for still wine are led by bacchus, frequently said to be England's answer to sauvignon blanc (a grape currently rarely planted here), followed by pinot gris.

Chardonnay is now comparatively easy to ripen in southern England. Similarly, pinot noir is fine for fizz almost every year, but it needs to grow on warm sites if it is regularly to become good still red wine. Pinot meunier splits opinions, yet some very attractive single-variety and blended wines, sparkling and still, are being made from it.

Bacchus was developed to flourish in cool northern Europe, but while many of its less satisfactory predecessors were hybrids it is pure *Vitis vinifera*, the true wine grape. Award-winning Sussex makers of aromatic, fresh and very enjoyable bacchus include Albourne, Bolney and Nutbourne.

Hybrid grape varieties can have odder flavours – seyval blanc is one that prompts violently different views, even being described as tasting of old potato and cabbage. But the sparkling versions made by Peter Hall at Breaky Bottom, tucked into the South Downs inland from Newhaven, are superb, with no hint at all of either vegetable.

Pinot gris and its sibling pinot blanc do very well in Sussex. Simon Woodhead at Stopham Estate near Pulborough makes excellent examples of both, and Bolney produces a multi-awarded pinot gris.

Slowly, more English dessert wines are appearing, even if most are from beyond Sussex borders. Early ripening, aromatic ortega, of German origin, is proving good for sweet wines, as is solaris, whose unusual grand-parentage includes an Asiatic wild red grape.

Speaking of red grapes, the champagne varieties apart, early-ripening, deep-coloured rondo is the most planted, but only in small quantities. There is even less dornfelder and regent, though the latter has some influential supporters. UK wine legislation puts very little restriction on which grapes are allowed to be planted, but the highest tier of the UK Quality Wine Scheme excludes use of hybrid varieties.

Left, chardonnay, pinot noir
Right, bacchus, pinot blanc

hours to set the fan going. At Ridgeview, a small trial of electric heating cables set along the trellis has proved encouraging, but this relies on a powerful enough power source nearby. In particularly wealthy parts of the wine world – though not, to my knowledge, in England – helicopters are chartered to disperse the cold air.

So if you're visiting in April and the everyone is looking bleary-eyed, be sympathetic. They could have been up at 4am, lighting bougies...

Inside: spreading the word beyond Britain

This month and next, Bolney continues to bottle the blended base wines that, after second fermentation, will become its sparkling wines; at Ridgeview this goes on through much of the year. Yet before the sparkling wines are finished and ready for sale there will be more to do (*see June*).

Spring is when the thoughts of both estates' sales teams turn to exports and they prepare for trips to potential buyers. Ridgeview's wines now sell in some twenty countries world-wide, Bolney's in ten, and a number will be visited each year. This contact is important, to explain the story of English sparkling wine.

Now is also the moment to talk to all commercial clients before they write their summer wine lists.

May
Outside: let in the air and sun

Even in May, frost is still a risk, so vineyard staff need to remain vigilant. Matt Strugnell recalls having to leave his cosy sleeping bag several times one very cold night (he'd taken time off to go on a camping trip) in order to find a strong enough phone signal to check the forecast and warn his colleagues when to light the bougies. Ridgeview is fortunate, however, as temperatures don't fall as low as they do in many other vineyards. It is easier to save the buds at minus 3°C than it is at minus 7°C. At Bolney, most of the vineyards slope enough for the frost to roll away, though a few need careful watching.

As the month progresses, the vines will have grown enough for the start of canopy management – controlling the density of shoots and leaves to keep good air movement around the developing bunches of grapes and allow sun through. Learning how to do this properly has hugely improved the quality of English wine, Bolney's Sam Linter emphasises. So in May, perhaps even in April, workers will be rubbing off surplus leaf buds and thinning shoots. Ridgeview contracts out this to Vine-Works; at Bolney, where there's a bigger vineyard team, staff do the work.

An important aim of canopy management is to avoid disease. It makes so much more sense, says Matt Strugnell, to prevent that rather than react once a problem strikes, when more powerful, more expensive chemical treatments are required. Once more, careful attention to weather forecasts is essential, to decide whether spraying should start: in certain conditions clean, healthy vines can rapidly become enveloped in a veil of mildew.

There are two main kinds, downy and powdery *(see September to learn about a third, botrytis)*. Both attack the leaves and other soft green parts of the plant, leading to poor fruit set. Powdery mildew also spoils the grapes, ruining the flavour of future wine.

Mildew isn't only a modern problem, as this illustration from a 19th century French treatise on vine diseases shows.

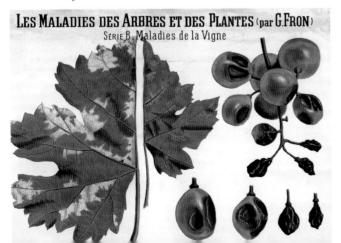

Just to make growers' lives even more difficult, while both mildews love shade they're contrary in other ways. If there's a hot spell, followed by significant rain, downy mildew strikes; if days become overcast, warm and humid, it's the turn of powdery (also known as oidium). And each needs a different deterrent treatment.

Spraying against disease is carefully controlled these days. Ridgeview pioneered the use in England of a recycling tunnel sprayer, and the current machine is remarkably precise. No liquid falls on the ground or spreads beyond the vines and excess spray is recovered. Early in the season, when leaf cover is low, as much as 85% is sucked back for reuse. Bolney has been using a similar sprayer since 2008.

Inside: debris with a welcome purpose

While still wines will, with few exceptions, be bottled in the spring or summer following harvest, sparkling wines wait patiently in cool cellars. The second fermentation results in a deposit of exhausted yeast cells in the bottle, and leaving the wine in contact with this debris is known as lees ageing. It imparts extra flavour and complexity.

At Ridgeview, the non-vintage wines – Bloomsbury, Cavendish, Fitzrovia – usually spend 12 to 18 months on their lees, to give depth to the characteristic fresh fruitiness. For the limited release vintage wines, that time will extend to three years, and for magnums it is a minimum of 10 years. Bolney's fizz is also lees-aged for 12 to 18 months, with five years plus for magnums.

Export and home sales visits begin now. The Scandinavian countries, where state monopolies run alcohol sales, make their decisions at this time of year, so reminding them of what Sussex can offer is important, says Simon Roberts.

Outside and in: welcome, everyone

Wine tourism increasingly carries on year round, but there is a highlight, English Wine Week. That normally happens at the end of May – Spring Bank Holiday week – and vineyards round the country lay on extra events. These can be extended tours or tastings, or more elaborate happenings such as pop-up restaurants, music among the vines, even demonstrations of slicing open a sparkling wine bottle with a sabre (yes, I've seen it done and very impressive it was).

Just in time, the latest vintage of still wines goes on sale.

June
Outside: the scent of summer

Have you ever smelt a vine flower? It's delicate, lightly honeyed, hinting at the liquid pleasures to come. But the

Sparkling wine production at Ridgeview: above, debris of dead yeast cells. below, bottles resting on their lees after second fermentation.
Photos by Misca Haller

A vine in flower at Ridgeview.

Tiny creature, massive damage

The ultimate nasty in a vineyard is the phylloxera louse, a root-nibbling bug that devastated Europe's vineyards in the late 19th century. It pops its ominous head up still, but is largely kept in check by grafting desired grape varieties on to phylloxera-resistant native American vine rootstock. That solution enabled the European wine industry to revive and survive. The 'dreaded' phylloxera was once common in many parts of the UK, if one 19th century winemaker is to be believed, but official records confirmed only a very few identifications. If it is still around – and it did make an appearance in Hampshire in the 1950s, on resistant, grafted vines – silence implies it isn't a current problem.

delicacy stretches beyond scent. If the weather is wrong – too wet or too windy – many flowers won't set into fruit and there will be fewer grapes, maybe hardly any, to harvest later. That happened in 2012, one of the wettest Junes ever recorded in England. Much of the rest of that year also saw pretty atrocious grape-growing weather and a miserable harvest all round. One much-publicised result was that Nyetimber made no wine at all.

Such extremes are an increasing risk as climate changes. No wonder that this is the time when every grower has fingers and toes crossed. 'We're hoping it doesn't rain,' says Ridgeview's Matt Strugnell. 'We're always hoping it doesn't rain!'

If the much-desired sunny weather doesn't happen, or disease strikes, there are two very visible results in the developing grape bunches. One is 'hen and chickens' or, more technically, millerandage. This is a mix of berry sizes in each bunch, bigger ones ready to develop normally alongside tiny ones that will never ripen fully. Coulure looks rather different: small berries fall off, leaving sparse bunches. Both can reduce yields significantly. Continuing canopy management is vital in ensuring good fruit set.

Something else that relies on good weather happens now: floral initiation. This is the formation of future fruit buds, in the joint between leaf and stem. A bad early summer will mean fewer grape bunches the following year – poor weather in 2011 was another of the factors that made the 2012 harvest such a disaster.

There are nasties in Sussex vineyards, as elsewhere in the UK: pests as well as diseases. Most pests are rather larger than the notorious phylloxera louse: from deer and rabbits tempted nibble vine trunks to wasps and birds that attack ripe fruit. High, deep-dug fences should keep out the animals; netting and noisy scarers can deter the feathered attackers, though nets are expensive, labour-intensive to install and can trap birds. So instead many growers accept some small loss of fruit.

But various moths, whose caterpillars eat into grapes causing damage and leading to rot, are an increasing problem. One unwelcome visitor at Ridgeview and, less frequently, at Bolney is the light brown apple moth, and ground-covering plants between the rows of vines that attract beneficial insects are a big help in controlling it. There are also biological aids against specific moth species – pheromone traps that attract the males and stop the moths reproducing. Bolney has camera traps among the vines to monitor moth activity and indicate when it is time to put the traps out.

Inside: now the debris must be removed
Final preparation of sparkling wine is in full swing. But before

Waiting for riddling and disgorgement: bottles at Bolney.
Photo by Chris Orange, www.chrisorange.com

crown caps can be replaced by corks, and all the smart labelling done, the yeast debris remaining from the second fermentation must be nudged into the neck of the bottle. That used to be a long, long process, the bottles set top down into slanting racks and rotated individually by hand, the angle steadily increasing each time, to encourage the sediment to lodge on the crown cork. It's known as riddling.

Since Spain's cava makers invented a mechanical alternative some 50 years ago, cellar workers suffer far fewer worn-out shoulders and wrists. The manual turning is replaced by machines: gyropalettes that hold some 500 bottles, rotating

Above, gyropalettes at Bolney (left) and Ridgeview. Below, from left, lifting riddled bottles, and bottles ready in line for disgorgement at Ridgeview; disgorgement completed at Bolney.

Ridgeview photos by XDB Photography and (bottle line) Emma Wood. Bolney photos by Toby Phillips Photography.

and upending them in a matter of days, with increasingly sophisticated automated controls.

After riddling, one more process awaits: disgorging, removal of the sediment. How can it be done without losing half the content of the bottle?

Some very skilled winemakers simply whip off the crown cap, letting only a tiny amount of wine plus debris to escape, and rapidly top up the bottle. Mostly, though, this process is also done mechanically. The bottle is upturned and its neck is plunged into liquid nitrogen or similar. Then it comes back upright, the crown cap is removed, a plug of frozen sediment pops out and the small volume of lost liquid is replaced.

What is added at this stage – the *dosage*, wine plus usually a little sweetener – determines the character of the final wine, from demi-sec (off dry) to brut or brut nature (little or no additional sweetness).

In goes the cork, a simple cylinder – the mushroom shape is created by the wire muzzle fitted on top to ensure the pressure inside the bottle doesn't push it off – and the bottle is dressed to kill. At Ridgeview, disgorgement carries on all through the year, three or four times a week; at Bolney, where production is split between still and sparkling, it is also a year-round activity, but a less frequent one.

Before leaving the winery, the finished sparkling wine is left to rest for a while, to ensure it is ready for buyers to enjoy immediately or later, as they prefer.

July
Outside: sizeable decisions
Flowering continues, and as the bunches of grapes develop they increasingly need to see the sun. So from late June and on into July excess shoot growth on the sides and tops of the vines is trimmed away, usually by machine. Once you understand the reason for it, you realise that this aspect of canopy management isn't simply expression of a tidy gardening mindset.

There is some hands-on work, too. Supporting wires are lifted, shoots are positioned vertically and some cut out if they are too close, further unwanted buds are rubbed away. Also, excess leaves around the bunches are pulled off. This is particularly important for red varieties to avoid the damaging attention of the spotted wing drosophila, a fruit fly unusual in

Too hungry to wait:
spotted wing drosophilia.
Photo by Shane McEvey

Time to visit the vines: a tour at Ridgeview. Photo by Julia Claxton

In the first the number of berries in a sample of bunches is counted and, as final berry weight falls within a fairly small range, a figure can be estimated for the whole plot. For average bunch weight, a number of partially-grown bunches are weighed and compared with figures from previous years at the same stage. Some more sums, and the likely harvest-time figure appears.

Is the crop so large that extra tanks will be needed? Is the potential harvest of pinot noir encouraging enough to consider buying barrels for still wine? Or is it going to be a poor year, so fewer seasonal workers will need to be recruited?

Outside and in: plenty for visitors to see and do

The vines are flourishing, hopefully the weather is good. Visiting a vineyard comes increasingly high on the list of summer tourist experiences. Picnics among the vines are popular: for them, Bolney and Ridgeview are among many estates offering hampers of local products. Tours range from a simple stroll to guided experiences ending in a sit-down tasting and food matching session or a meal. Every vineyard that welcomes visitors has a website listing what's going on and most have email newsletters, or search at winegb.co.uk. Even those too young to taste are welcomed: there's a prize for every child who successfully finds Bertie the Bolney Bunnie.

that it doesn't wait for its meal to be fully cooked – it attacks grapes as they ripen.

As flowering ends, vineyard managers make their initial estimate of the size of the crop. That's never easy, and many later factors will affect the result, but the estimate allows preliminary planning in the winery. There are, explains Matt Strugnell, two ways of arriving at reasonably accurate figures: berry count and average bunch weight.

August

Outside: look what's happening to the grapes

This month sees a crucial stage for the growing grapes: veraison, when red grapes start to show the first signs of their final colour. More than that is happening, though. All the grapes, whatever colour, are swelling, their skins are softening and the sugars inside are increasing. Again, veraison is most successful when the weather is dry and warm and canopy trimming lets in the sun.

Now there's another practice that helps the crop – the perhaps surprising one of cutting off some of the bunches of grapes. This 'green harvesting' is intended to ensure each vine has the right quantity of grapes to ripen well. Leaving too many grapes where vines yield generously means they will take longer to ripen, or perhaps never ripen quite enough. In England, a serious surfeit of bunches doesn't happen often and green harvesting can be as much about disease control as keeping the crop to a particular level. If bunches are too crowded rot may start, and spread.

While canopy management has stopped, there is still much else going on. Development of the grapes is constantly monitored and a lookout is kept for disease or pest problems.

For companies such as Ridgeview, which bring in grapes from partner growers, it's time to assess their crops – so Matt

Why ripeness matters

Every effort to encourage ripeness is crucial. Remember those earlier references to the 'lean, mean' wines of the past – much of the problem was that grapes simply weren't properly ripe.

Why does that matter? Well, the juice of unripe grapes has very high levels of acidity. Plenty of acidity is valuable in sparkling wines, but in still wines too much makes for a mouth-puckering experience. The winemaking process can counter this, but the results are never as good as those from fully ripened grapes.

In addition, wine essentially needs to include alcohol, which results when yeast acts on the sugars in grape juice during fermentation; the more sugar the higher the potential alcohol. Alcohol adds warmth and rounds out the flavours.

Until comparatively recently (and even now in a few cases) many English wines had single-figure alcohol levels. Reasonably palatable low alcohol wines can be made now, but for most consumers any dry wine below around 11% alcohol is hard going.

So having grapes ripe enough to produce natural alcohol levels of 12% or 13% is an important advance and means less sugary intervention is needed before fermentation – increasing numbers of English wines now need none at all. In 2020 there were reports of grapes being picked, though in Essex not Sussex, with a potential natural alcohol level of 15%, extraordinary for England.

Strugnell is off on a tour round them all. Back home, he starts to prepare for harvest, as do fellow vineyard managers round the county. All the necessary equipment – trailers, crates, buckets, snips (harvesting secateurs), etc – has to be checked and pickers booked.

Inside: deciding how much crop to expect

Winemakers should already have a good idea of the size of the crop to expect. That's down to the vineyard managers' initial estimates from flowering time *(see July)*, plus adjustments as the grapes ripen.

With harvest approaching, there is plenty of last-minute preparation. Picking crates must be cleaned and placed ready

Are these grapes ripe? Matt Strugnell tests sugar levels in chardonnay with a refractometer.

among the vines, all the equipment the pickers need prepared, tractors checked. Final cleaning ensures a spotless winery, essential if quality wine is to be made.

September

Outside: ripeness is crucial

Before harvesting can start, the grapes must be ripe. Different varieties will reach optimum ripeness at different times, though the window is quite limited. Grapes for still wines, such as bacchus, ripen soonest and will be the first to be picked. Those intended for sparkling wine are harvested at slightly lower ripeness levels; pinot noir will normally be ready before chardonnay. Grapes destined for sweet wine will be picked last – maybe into November.

How is ripeness assessed? Obviously, the look of the grapes helps – hard green berries clearly won't be ready. There are both natural and scientific methods to help the grower decide. Many vineyard managers simply taste the grapes, though it takes years of experience to judge them well, and most also use a sugar-monitoring refractometer.

Sugar is only part of the story. The pips need to be ripe, otherwise there will be a vegetal edge to the flavour of the pressed juice. Green stalks present a similar problem. Tannins, which give character to red wines, also need to lose their earlier astringency. So if you hear talk of 'phenolic' or 'physiological' ripeness it means growers are considering much more than the sweetness of grape flesh and juice. The chemistry is complicated, one reason why Plumpton and other agricultural colleges offer specialist wine courses, to degree or master level.

Let the grapes get too ripe, however, and they lose acidity, essential both for the particular character of English still wine and for quality sparkling wine.

When both taste and sugar content look good, it's time to be much more technical. A small number of bunches of each variety are collected and analysed in the winery laboratory, for precise assessment of potential alcohol and acid levels. If these are right, let harvest begin.

In Sussex vineyards, and through the rest of the UK, almost all harvesting is by hand. It is required under the rules for classic method sparkling wines, where whole bunches go into the press rather than the individual berries that mechanical grape picking machines shake off the vines.

But machines are coming: one of England's biggest producers, Denbies in Surrey, has been using one for several years. In 2019 Bolney experimented successfully on a very small scale, and expanded the harvest area in 2020. 'From our trial use, subsequent still wines we produced showed that there was no compromises in quality or any consequences for the

Above, a harvesting machine in action at Bolney in 2020 – for grapes intended for still wine only. But cutting the grapes by hand, right, won't stop (photo by Graeme Robertson).

winemaking process,' Sam Linter reports. 'If anything, the fruit was delivered cleaner, and fresher. But hand picking will, of course, still continue.'

Not many years ago, harvest in Sussex didn't start until well into October. That's changed a lot. In 2020, many growers began picking in the third week of September, the earliest ever for many of them. And most were finished before mid-October. Even in less favourable summers, harvest begins at least a fortnight earlier than ten or even five years ago.

Is this down to a warming climate, even though the huge variability in English weather brings problems as well as advantages? Or are other factors – notably human ones – more important? From his long experience at Ridgeview, Matt Strugnell believes earlier harvests are down to a combination of climate change and improvement in grape growing. At Bolney, too, the effect of higher temperatures is acknowledged, alongside the significant difference made by the improved vineyard knowledge and practices.

Inside: here come the grapes...
In England, grapes arrive at the winery at a sensible time of day, unlike hot places where white grapes need to be harvested in the cool of the night and rushed to the winery before the dumbing effect of oxidation sets in, compromising freshness

Natural practice in the winery

After decades of organic standards for grape growing but none for wine making, that deficit was corrected in 2012, thanks to European legislation that banned the use of many synthetic products in the winery, limited additives and reduced permitted sulphur dioxide levels in the wines. But as with all wine making, individuals choose their own way within the rules.

Kristin Syltevik of Oxney Organic Estate in East Sussex believes that 'a very natural approach to winemaking' is most important. 'Let the vineyard talk – minimal sulphur dioxide, minimal filtration, minimal use of products/fining.' Organic principles are behind all she does – including 'recycling, reusing and repurposing as much as we can' – and a biomass boiler that provides heat for winemaking.

She notes with some satisfaction that an American comparative study found wine magazine critics' scores for organic wines were higher than for non-organic ones. 'This is probably because winemakers making organic wine take more care – they can't afford to make a mistake as they can't use, or don't want to use, various correcting products.'

and flavour. Minimal grape miles are essential in those circumstances. Here, it's rather different.

The crop can travel long distances: one winery in Devon makes great wine from grapes grown in Essex. Journeys are normally much shorter in Sussex, but even so Ridgeview brings in grapes from growers across the south of England, Nyetimber has vineyards in Kent as well as Sussex, and there are other county-spanning operations. But a lot of care is taken along the way. To avoid unwanted crushing, most grapes are picked directly into plastic crates holding a maximum of 12 kilos, and stay in them until they arrive at the winery.

There, they are checked, particularly if they come from other growers. Spraying residues, for example, are something no winemaker wants. Sometimes, the grapes will be decanted on to a sorting table or conveyor belt and unwanted bits and pieces, from rotten berries to caterpillars, removed. Next, it's into the press.

All quality-oriented wineries go to huge lengths to ensure damaging oxygen doesn't reach the fresh juice. Slatted wooden presses used to be traditional for sparkling wine, but pneumatic alternatives are popular now. Some spread a layer of inert gas, usually nitrogen, over their contents, to avoid oxidation. Whatever style of wine is made in England, gentle pressing is

essential, to prevent unwanted green flavours in the juice. Then comes fermentation.

October
Outside: the longest days

Harvest is continuing. Depending on the size of the vineyard, the varieties of vines and the workforce available, it can be finished in a few days or extend for several weeks.

At Ridgeview there are only five hectares of vineyard at the estate and with Vine-Works pickers doing the job the 2020 harvest was over in three days. At Bolney, the harvest generally lasts for three weeks, but again 2020's was finished unusually quickly.

Left, botrytis, unwanted except on grapes for sweet wine. Right, rot-free pinot noir harvested at Ridgeview (photo by XDB Photography).

The grapes arrive... Top row, sorting red and white at Bolney *(photo by Julia Claxton)*, and the winery's newest press *(photo by Vanessa Berberian)*; bottom row, from left, pinot noir goes into the press at Ridgeview *(photo by XDB Photography)* and the juice leaves it, ready for fermentation in the winery's stainless steel tanks and oak barrels *(photo by Julia Claxton)*.

All eyes remain on the weather forecast. Dry weather is obviously best, not only for the grapes but also for those who pick them. If showers drench the bunches immediately before picking time, there's little problem. But if the weather is warm and wet for several days furry *Botrytis cinerea* begins to grow, especially if the grape skins have been damaged by birds or insects or have burst when tight bunches expand. This grey mould rapidly makes the grapes useless for wine. Unless it comes later...

Then botrytis is the dream partner for any maker of sweet wine. When the grapes are healthy and autumn offers classic conditions of misty mornings and warm dry afternoons this 'noble rot' shrivels the grapes, concentrating juice and sugar and adding a marmalade-like tang. Wines created from such horrid-looking grapes are famous and cherished: Sauternes is the ultimate expression. Some such special sweet wines are starting to be made in England.

The busiest time in the vineyard year is reaching its end. 'The build-up to harvest is really nerve-wracking,' says Matt Strugnell, who also has to organise the schedule of picking at partner growers. His team and that at Bolney breathe huge sighs of relief when all the grapes are picked and pressed. By the end of the month, those 12- to 14-hour days are a fading memory...

Inside: bubble, bubble, hopefully no trouble

Except in unusually warm summers, the bulk of the grapes now arrive in the winery. At Ridgeview, grapes come in from partner growers over several weeks, and ensuring a steady stream is part of the essential planning. Vineyards further east – in Kent or Essex – usually harvest first, with Sussex and Hampshire sites somewhat later, though in 2020 'everyone wanted to pick at the same time', says Simon Roberts. That meant all the grapes arrived in four weeks rather than the usual eight and life in the winery was exceptionally busy.

After the gentle pressing is finished, the grape juice is left to settle for 24 to 36 hours. Then it is inoculated with wine yeast, necessary to turn the sugars in the grapes into alcohol. While some winemakers, especially organic growers, prefer to let fermentation happen naturally, with the yeasts that occur on grape skins and even linger in the winery, that takes courage. Most prefer to use a prepared yeast that will help towards the desired flavours and ensure the bubbling process of fermentation is steady and controlled.

Most English wines, certainly whites, are fermented at low temperatures (usually below 18°C), to protect the delicate scents and flavours. That will take two to three weeks.

If potential alcohol levels are too low, the solution is simple Just add sugar to the grape juice (there are limits set on how much) before fermentation, a practice known as chaptalisation. It is widespread in cool-climate wineries, and properly done produces very acceptable results.

As the main fermentation, with or without extra sugar, ends the moment arrives to decide whether to allow malolactic fermentation. This converts sharp malic acid in the juice into softer lactic acid and can be prompted by bacteria occurring naturally or deliberately introduced.

Simon Roberts prefers to put most of Ridgeview's base wines through malolactic fermentation, but in very ripe years malic acid may be naturally low and the intervention will lead to too flabby a result. Picking before acidity drops away is the ideal.

November
Outside: pruning can start
There's plenty of tidying-up to do after harvest, cleaning and storing away crates and machinery, and necessary jobs such as trellis repairs – providing it hasn't rained so much that it's too muddy to work among the vines.

As the month moves on, the vines lose their leaves. At this point, winter pruning begins at Bolney, though many estates wait until December, perhaps even January *(see January for the why and how of what happens)*. The early start at Bolney allows

the vineyard team to cover the whole of the estate without outside help.

Harder work than cutting is pulling the cut branches away from the wires and dropping them to the ground – Ridgeview employs contractors Vine-Works for that, while at Bolney they are turned into mulch by the estate's mower / mulcher machine.

When I talked to Matt Strugnell in November 2020 he was spending much more time than he liked in the office: all kinds of administrative work, budget planning, revising risk assessments, developing Ridgeview's programme to achieve the Sustainable Wine GB certification (work on Bolney's was similarly ongoing). But as well as being vineyard manager he is in charge of the whole estate, so there is time outside, taking

Racking in Bolney's winery.

Winter at Bolney.

care of woodland, ditch clearing, even landscaping around the new winery building.

Inside: racking isn't torture

By now some of the new wines will have completed their fermentation, but there is more to do before they are ready for bottling.

From the fermentation tank they are usually moved to a settling tank, where the solid particles of dead yeast and other by-products – known as lees – fall to the bottom and the clearer liquid is drawn off, the 'racking' process. Sometimes, to enhance flavours especially in finer wines, this contact with the lees continues for weeks or months, with stirring to increase the effect.

Towards the end of the month the pressure starts to ease. But there's plenty to keep other indoors staff busy, with the Christmas sales effort building – restaurants, bars and pubs are stocking up and consumers are tempted by a myriad of seasonal offers. This month, Bolney holds an annual Christmas fair, inviting local food producers and crafts people.

December

Outside: keep the wellies on

If you're new to vineyard work, you'd hope this would be the one month to take time off. But no. The post-harvest clearing has to be finished, and if winter pruning didn't start in November it will do so now. Back on with the wellies...

Inside: vermouth and gin as well as wine

With fermentation finished, racking continues and the remaining pre-bottling processes for still wines begin (*go to January to learn about those*). Blending of still wines and of base wines for fizz starts. Also, at Bolney the embryo rondo and dornfelder wine goes through micro-oygenation. where a tiny, controlled amount of oxygen is passed through the fermented juice, softening tannins and making the wine smoother.

Among festive offerings from Sussex vineyards are drinks beyond wine. Bolney's Rosso was the first Sussex red vermouth, estate red wine fortified and blended with locally picked sloes and elderberries. Sam Linter is delighted to have found a use for those fruits the birds ignore. Another Sussex vermouth – very pale amber this time and off dry rather than dry – is Albourne's 40, the number reflecting the herbs and spices in the blend.

There is gin, too, made from Sussex-grown grapes.

Bolney's comes from the final part of the estate's press juice, which isn't good enough to become wine. It is distilled with delicate botanical flavourings including hawthorn leaves from the hedgerows surrounding the vines.

As December continues, thoughts turn naturally to sparkling wine, and there's a final rush on sales. English sparkling wine may be bottled during most of the year, but the largest number of corks are pulled in December. Happy Christmas, happy new year!

Ready for the Christmas buying rush at Ridgeview.
Photo by XDB Photography

Chapter 4

Stages towards success

When you ask any independent winemakers, anywhere, what they want their wines to show off the answers are predictable and often identical. Place / terroir / grape...

'I've always wanted our wine to be true to its roots, to respect the fruit character, I've never wanted to play with it too much,' is Sam Linter's take on that. 'We do aim for balance: balance between acidity, mouthfeel, alcohol, sugar. If you get that right the wine really sings.'

That balance was, she admits, difficult to achieve in the 1990s and the very early 2000s. But experience has shown Bolney's winemaking team the right varieties to plant, and longer, warmer summers have brought riper grapes from them. Crucially, good wine results from good work in the vineyard. 'It's all about pruning, canopy management, talking to the people who work with the vines. We are just caretakers of the product we get in.'

Sam, like so many of her counterparts in English vineyards, learnt much of her winemaking skill at Plumpton College. As mother of two young children, she studied part time and there was no chance of travelling to other wine countries. Then – the late 1990s – Plumpton's courses were far from the comprehensive degrees offered now. For example, she was taught nothing about sparkling wine making.

'I learnt a lot from other people,' she explains, citing one colleague who spent half the year at Bolney, the other half at an innovative, pioneering winery in Marlborough, New Zealand. 'She'd come back with all the ideas that were going on in the new world.'

Mike Roberts at Ridgeview, 'an amazing man', was an invaluable mentor when she decided to make a sparkling wine for the millennium. The only information she could find was in French, which she couldn't read. Patiently, Mike explained technical processes such as *tirage* (the stage where yeast and sweetener is added to the still base wine to prompt second fermentation in bottle) time and again – and again after she got home and realised she still didn't fully understand what to do.

'Without him, Bolney would not have started making sparkling wine as early as we did.'

The flavours in the bottles

How do wines made in Sussex taste? Every wine tastes different to every drinker, so it's near impossible to define individual bottles. But there are general characteristics. Before you read on, an admission: these aren't my descriptions of aroma and taste. They are those (gently edited) that were submitted to the European Commission as part of the application process for the Sussex Protected Designation of Origin, about which you'll find more in Chapter 6.

Sparkling wines first: 'The cooler climate and longer growing season gives crisp lemon citrus and green apple acidity to the chardonnays, while the pinots can have a more earthy mix of red berry and baked apple flavours, producing wines that are clean and fresh, yet have depth and are complex, with richness in character.

'The longer on-lees bottle ageing produces wines with fresh toast, melon, baked brioche and honey aromas on the nose and palate. All the wines demonstrate a fine and persistent mousse.'

Now the still ones, where again the cool climate and long growing season are a big influence, leading to 'wines with prominent floral and fruit-driven flavours'.

'Characteristics such as lemon, lime, elderflower and other floral notes, apple, pear and gooseberry are strongly apparent in the white wines. Rosé wines can be delicate and floral with hints of white flowers, rose petals, melon and strawberry. Reds will generally be lighter in style with soft tannins and hints of red and black fruits, leather, juicy plums and wild berry on the palate.'

But perhaps she still didn't fully understand... The warning came when the crown cork of a bottle from that inaugural batch popped off during second fermentation. She checked another: the pressure was nine bars, almost double the desired norm. Quickly, all remaining bottles were carried to the middle of the vineyard for safe opening. 'I'd made 300 little bombs!'

For a newcomer to one of the most technical aspects of winemaking it was, she admits, very easy to get the enrichment calculations wrong. 'The good news is that the mistake will never be repeated.'

Few avoid at least one geyser of wine

Not all errors in the winery are as explosive as that, but few winemakers have avoided the geyser that erupts when insufficient head space is left in a fermentation tank. At Bolney many years ago a cellar assistant rushed to the office shouting there had been a 'terrible accident' – fortunately an overexaggeration. Sam found her assistant winemaker perched on top of a tank in a little Dutch boy/finger in the dyke effort to stop the fermenting wine pouring out. 'It happens once in a winemaker's life, and you learn not to do it again.'

Pleasures far outweigh such downsides, she emphasises: 'Wine is amazing, absolutely fascinating: it gets addictive. How do you walk away from working in the wine trade?'

Simon Roberts agrees: 'Winemaking is something you do because you have the passion for it. That's something we all share.'

While Sam Linter has worked entirely in England, Michael Hayward, her deputy and production manager, introduces some broader experience. He worked in the winery of a Tuscan estate for a year, where red varieties including sangiovese and pinot noir were the main focus, before taking first class honours in a wine production degree at Plumpton and joining Bolney in 2015.

His aim there is that both still and sparkling wines 'should be vibrant and fresh – I don't think England should be afraid of complementary acidity, because it is a nice point of difference'.

At Bolney, still wine remains predominant, almost 60 per cent of production. 'We see ourselves as still wine specialists; we aspire to be the premier still wine grower in the UK, to remain true to our roots,' says Sam.

As I write, early in 2021, there are two still reds, three still whites, a still rosé and eight sparklers (one of those, most unusually, is red). Sam suggests the range may be a little too wide, but there are markets for them all so it's hard to lose a wine from the list and disappoint its supporters.

There's always work to do in the winery. This is Ridgeview's.

Michael Hayward adds: 'All our still wines have steadily improved, due to the attention that has been placed on to them. With our sparkling wine, we're always going to treasure the magic of making a great blanc de blancs, but for me, there is so much scope in the world of still wines, and I think the UK will end up going that way.'

Ridgeview's range has, from the early days, been built around the most classic sparkling wine styles – until the arrival of the limited-production 25th birthday Oak Reserve. Doing something new takes a long time. 'You cannot rush things,' emphasises Simon Roberts. Much of the experimentation in the winery is linked to such seemingly minor items as corks – important for the quality of the wine, yet way beyond the interest of most of those who drink it. 'We're always tweaking things. We trial everything, and that generally takes two to three years. It's all very geeky.'

Ridgeview's inaugural trio, Bloomsbury (one of the Queen's Diamond Jubilee wines and the classic blend of chardonnay, pinot noir and pinot meunier), Cavendish (the same trio of grapes, but with the reds taking precedence) and Fitzrovia Rosé (served to US President Barack Obama at Buckingham Palace) remain the excellent-value signature range. From 2009 to 2016 they were joined by Knightsbridge blanc de noirs, Grosvenor blanc de blancs and Victoria rosé de noirs, a higher tier though still approachably priced.

With the introduction of the new wines came the decision to move Bloomsbury, Cavendish and Fitzrovia to non vintage, creating a consistent house brand, and then to replace the newer wines' London titles with immediately understandable blend names. These – Blanc de Blancs, Blanc de Noirs and Rosé de Noirs – continue as vintage wines. A total rebranding in 2018 gave all the bottles a stylish, contemporary aspect.

Stylishly dressed: Ridgeview's rebranded vintage range.

Wines with other labels

For both Ridgeview and Bolney, making wine under contract for other growers is an important part of the business. There are far more vineyards than wineries in England: the 2020 figure was 770 of the former, 165 of the latter. As a result, many growers rely on winemakers happy to process more than their own harvest.

At Bolney, contract winemaking is on the rise again, as since the opening of the new winery in 2019 there is potential to grow that back towards the 40 per cent of production it used to be. Most contract customers are small growers. The smallest usually want no more than a straightforward wine with their name on the label; larger ones, some trained winemakers themselves, often like to have more input in what goes on, and to experiment – which Sam enjoys, though she has yet to be asked to make an example of newly fashionable orange wine.

At Ridgeview, rather the reverse is happening. As the brand grows, contract production is likely to drop, to below the current level of about a third of the total. But it certainly won't stop.

For Simon Roberts, interaction with contract customers is part of the winemaking pleasure. Some make contact only distantly, but others want to be very much involved all the way through the process. He likes the latter approach: 'Grape growing is key to making wine and that is their part of the journey. We are creating a product for their brand. We get to share in their journey.'

2020, above, was the earliest harvest on record at Bolney, as at many other Sussex estates (photo by Julia Claxton) – but not as generous as 2018, below.

Satisfaction: Ridgeview's 2020 harvest. Photo by XDB Photography

The relationship with both contract customers and partner growers is very important, Simon emphasises. 'We don't make wine for just anyone. We have to have a very close relationship.' Sometimes, there can be complicated discussions, especially if the raw material isn't as good as it should be.

'Generally, if we suggest something they think it is a good idea...'

Contract customers rarely take Bolney's Michael Hayward out of his comfort zone, though he argues: 'If I don't make wines that I want to drink, I'm not going to be making the best possible wine.' But he's relaxed about what goes on. 'They have as much say as they like. Some people put complete trust in our winemaking, other customers like to retain artistic licence. I'm happy both ways!'

Every year is different

One continuing issue with making wine even in sunny Sussex is the variability of vintages. Growers have long accepted that there will be years where the weather makes a decent grape harvest impossible – a couple in every decade has been the usual estimate. But in the years that have followed the disaster of 2012, they've been smiling.

The vintage of 2018 will long go down in memory as magnificent, with a record quantity of grapes, of very high quality. The following year was pretty good, too, though nothing like as generous.

Then 2020 came along. For many growers it was their earliest-ever harvest, starting in mid September. The grapes were perfectly ripe. They were small – not so good for volume (though given the constraints forced by the coronavirus pandemic on work in vineyard and winery that was no bad thing) but excellent for quality.

'With small berries you get concentrated sugars but you can get really high acids as well. This year we had such warm nights the acidity is balanced,' Sam Linter told me as we looked out over the golden, ready-to-pick chardonnay. 'I wouldn't be surprised if quality exceeds 2018 – and 2018 was the best ever.'

So what more appropriate moment to learn which are the favourite wines, and the food to go with them, of the people who grow the grapes, make the wines and run Bolney and Ridgeview.

The wines their producers like best

Sam Linter says her favourite changes with her mood, but when I insist, she singles out Bolney Pinot Noir. 'I obviously love the grape variety, it's fascinating, with so much versatility. There is red cherry when first bottled, couple of years later savoury notes come in. The evolution is quite dramatic.'

She drinks it with cheese – brie is a first choice – and also, surprisingly, with asparagus. 'Duck and asparagus is the perfect match.'

There is also a family tradition: Bolney Bubbly on Fridays. 'It's fun and so easy to drink. We drink on its own, but it goes

Add food, for extra pleasure.

with quite a lot.' Salmon tagliatelle with tarragon cream and lemon is a favourite pairing.

For Tamara Roberts, to choose just one wine is a challenge. 'It depends so much on mood, company and occasion. I have been surprised just how well our wines go with a wide range of cuisine.

'Perhaps one of my favourite experiences was at a meal with our Dutch importers and we discovered that our rosé, Ridgeview Fitzrovia, was the perfect match across all of the courses, and we certainly tried quite a few other wines before reaching that decision!'

Graham Linter votes for Bolney Lychgate Red (rondo and dornfelder, with a little pinot noir). 'It goes really well with a roast, but is also great for drinking on its own in the evening.'

Simon and Mardi Roberts share the same favourite: the Ridgeview Oak Reserve NV. 'It is one of the loveliest wines I have ever tasted,' says Mardi, always a fan of oaked wines. 'It's such a complete glass.' Simon Roberts enjoys the richness – and the fact that it is new to the estate portfolio.

Their food partner for it is again unanimous: Christmas lunch with all the trimmings. 'That's my favourite meal of the year,' adds Simon.

Chris Roberts' choice is Ridgeview Blanc de Blancs. 'I'd go for something delicate like salmon with it and thoroughly enjoy both.'

Charlotte Linter is adamant: 'It's got to be the Cuvée Noir (Bolney's classic method bubbly red, made from dornfelder). It's so unusual and interesting and I really enjoy it with Goupie cherry and almond chocolates (sold on the estate's website).'

Matt Strugnell retains a very soft spot for Cavendish 1998, the first Ridgeview wine he tasted. 'I thought wow, this is amazing.' But from the current wines it has to be Rosé de Noirs, 'a knock-out with roast lamb'.

Simon Larder loves Ridgeview Cavendish NV 'all the way'. Approachable, not expensive, the perfect present. 'It's just fantastic.' And try this for an exotic food match: sticky chilli tofu. 'It might be a challenge...'

Michael Hayward puts Bolney's Pinot Gris top of his list. 'I think it's a brilliant wine, unique, and with the warm summers it's only going to get better. As a winemaking team we have some interesting plans for this grape variety in the future.' Perfect partner, he says, is roast chicken.

Chapter 5

Will there ever be too much?

In 2018, vineyard owners in Sussex – and throughout the rest of England – faced a very unusual but ultimately happy situation. A frost-free spring, perfect flowering season, warm summer and dry harvest period, plus new vines coming into production, brought a bumper harvest, the biggest ever. The UK-wide result was some 13.1 million bottles of wine, well over double the average of the previous five years.

Before any wine was made, there were all sorts of problems: the extra number of people needed to pick the grapes; the places to put them – wineries rushed to buy more and more fermentation and storage vats, with even empty milk tankers pressed into use when more conventional containers overflowed; the ability to cope with so much more fruit than usual during every stage of winemaking. And that wasn't the end of the matter. There's a very important question: will all those bottles, the 10.5 million from 2019 that followed them and the increasing number from succeeding vintages, find ready buyers?

The market for English wine is growing, but only slowly,

Ridgeview

Just some of the hundreds of thousands of vines recently planted in Sussex. This is Mannings Heath in spring 1917.

were sold, little more than half of that year's production. And a sobering fact is that, in the UK, the home product accounts for less than two per cent of all wine sales.

Vineyard area has grown hugely recently: in 2017 a million vines were planted, in 2018 another 1.6 million, 2019 saw 3.2 million more, and a further million-plus joined them in 2020. Between 2010 and 2020, vineyard area increased by 150%, to a little over 3,500 hectares. Many of those expanding hectares of vines are not yet producing crops, or the early vintages of sparkling wines from them have yet to be released.

Soon there will be even more English wine ready to be sold. Who will buy it? Many eyes are looking towards export. Some ten per cent of total production already leaves UK shores, with the USA – notably California and New York – plus Canada and Norway the top destinations.

Both Ridgeview and Bolney sell their wines around the world, respectively around ten and five per cent of production. Early on, Ridgeview was fortunate. 'Export came to us,' explains Mardi Roberts – the catalyst was choice of Grosvenor Blanc de Blancs as Best International Sparkling Wine in the 2010 Decanter World Wine Awards. That was very special recognition, of which Simon Roberts is particularly proud, because the category included champagne as well as contenders from all the rest of the world.

and currently there is a big gap between sales and production (though this is partly accounted for by the ageing time needed for sparkling wines). For example, in 2019 5.5 million bottles

Mardi argues that selling abroad, as a premium product, will encourage producers to continue to make the highest quality wines, rather than lowering their ambitions and ending up in a home price war. 'It's about ensuring the future of Ridgeview and of English sparkling wine.'

Sam Linter would love to broaden Bolney's markets, but 'you have to travel – it's incredibly expensive'. Most individual producers have to rule that out on cost-effective grounds, so it needs collective effort. There's a WineGB export committee aiming to prompt and co-ordinate that.

But even a substantial increase in exports won't be enough. It's up to the vineyards themselves, the regional producer groups and the trade body to encourage more people in the UK to drink local. There is one vital way. 'We need to get people to taste it,' says Mardi Roberts. 'So they don't have to take our word for it.'

Ridgeview has long encouraged tastings – and all its early consumer comparisons were done blind, with glasses of its wine set alongside champagne and fine fizz from elsewhere in the world, all unidentified. No need to guess which wine was frequently the favourite. Though Mike Roberts used to recount that the tasters often told him they wanted to change their opinion once they realised that they had preferred English bubbles to those best-known the world over...

'We never wanted to say we were better than champagne, but that we could stand side by side,' Mardi emphasises. Interestingly, she reveals that the name Ridgeview was deliberately chosen because it could be taken as originating from places other than England. 'On the first labels there was just a little "UK" at the bottom.' As Mike had insisted, the taste, not the location, should be England's unique selling point.

Some good came out of bad

No-one is happy to say good things about a pandemic, but Covid-19 helped to boost English wine sales direct to

Covid-19 ended vineyard tours, such as this one at Bolney.

Ridgeview's Wine Garden. Photo by XDB Photography

consumers, reinforcing an already expanding enthusiasm for minimum food and drink miles and for staycation wine tourism.

Beforehand, many producers were competently showing how to win support, and sales, with direct approaches to consumers. Now, that is ever more important. But the thinking needs to go broader. 'It's all about spreading where you sell your wines, not having your eggs all in one basket,' Sam Linter stresses. Mike Roberts had always said the same.

From early on in the sparkling wine revolution, restaurants have been the major outlet – because sommeliers can explain the background to the bottles and argue their champagne-equalling quality. In March 2020, Covid-19 abruptly shut down that on-trade market, and wine producers throughout England suddenly took a huge hit on their income. And that happened again and again, with succeeding waves of the virus.

'Not everyone could pay for the wine they'd taken, so you weren't being paid for months,' Sam Linter explains. 'It was really difficult to manage that, but you could understand – the people in the on-trade weren't getting any money in either.'

Other sources of income collapsed, too, as vineyard tours and tasting experiences were halted. That's when websites became increasingly important. Anyone following English wine saw their in-box filling up with offers of specially selected cases, tempting discounts, free delivery. There was a massive and positive reaction.

Somewhat tongue-in-cheek, Simon Roberts reveals that Ridgeview suddenly saw a 2,000 per cent increase in on-line sales. 'But we weren't starting from a very large base...'

There are longer-term effects. For instance, Bolney now has a much wider offering both online and on-site. During lockdown, the estate shop expanded to include fresh produce boxes and meals prepared by the café's chef, available for local people to collect, with thank-you discounts for NHS workers.

Ridgefest: wines, vines and music. Photo by Julia Claxton

Since then it has extended its choice of local food products and matched them to bottles in an increasing variety of hampers of wine with cheese or charcuterie, picnic boxes, even a fizz-and-cream tea to enjoy at home. Customers signed up on the website receive frequent updates.

Generally, involvement with the local community leads to notice further afield, as Bolney found with its lockdown essential food boxes, and that helps to raise the profile of both producer and county. Other contact brings more attention close to home – for example, Nutbourne Vineyards' recruitment point for grape pickers has been the notice board at the village post office, and resulting enthusiasm prompted nearby farm shops and grocers specialising in local products to sell the estate's wines. Many producers encourage local restaurants and pubs to serve their wines, often by the glass so the introductory price isn't too high.

Individual initiatives apart, broader events reach a wider public. Inevitably, the annual English Wine Week had to be cancelled in 2020, meaning no guided tours through the vines, tasting sessions, wine-matching dinners or any of the other special events during this major annual 'welcome to the vineyards' event.

But the enterprising wine estates of Sussex still made the week memorable. Those who are part of Sussex Modern – which links and promotes the arts, landscape and winemaking in the county – put together celebratory mixed cases of their wines. Some vineyards, among them Albourne and Rathfinny, offered pre-booked picnics to collect and eat among the vines.

For virtual visitors free online wine-tasting experiences launched at Mannings Heath, linking to cellar master Johann Fourie in South Africa; Cherie Spriggs and Brad Greatrix hosted a 'meet the winemakers' session from Nyetimber; Sam Linter led a virtual tour round the Bolney Estate culminating in a tasting; Ridgeview offered a video glimpse behind the scenes to all online customers as well as running Zoom seminars and masterclasses. And that's only a snapshot of what happened.

The Bolney shop.

Some of these initiatives have become a lasting legacy. The very enthusiastic reaction to Bolney's virtual tastings is one example, prompting their more permanent addition to the attraction list.

As vineyard shops opened again, buyers returned. At Bolney, post-first-lockdown sales fully made up for those lost during four months when the door was shut. 'It was almost too busy in a way,' was Sam Linter's cheerful reaction.

A specially personal service

It's a pleasure to see how very personal the cellar-door service can be. On one of my visits to Ridgeview a couple in the shop hesitantly asked if a vintage to mark a special birthday was still available. It wasn't in the normal stock – but the immediate reaction from Mardi Roberts was an offer to search in hidden corners of the cellar. I don't know the result, but those customers will surely come back for the next memorable date.

Certainly, there will be more for them to enjoy. During the pandemic a lot of effort went into ensuring Ridgeview was a safe place to visit – but not just once. Mardi explains how wine tourists used to come a single time, with no incentive to return other than to buy another bottle or two. Creating the Wine Garden, though, changed that – offering the chance to try a line-up of wines, match them with food, picnic with baskets of local produce, enjoy the food from pop-up chefs, all socially distanced.

That effort, notes Simon Roberts, prompted plenty of customers to come back, sometimes weekend after weekend. Ridgeview is capitalising on it, with latest major investment the creation of a hospitality space within part of what was the old winery, and a new indoor/outdoor building at the Wine Garden. Ridgefest, the annual music among the vines festival, is back in the calendar – with attendances anticipated to touch 1,000. 'The whole cellar door experience is going to be a huge focus over the next few years,' he adds.

Charlotte Linter agrees. 'I think that being able to come to the Bolney estate, meet the team and see the beauty and magic of the vineyards, really helps the customer feel more emotionally connected to our products. It gives us the chance to share our passion and our story, by being able to show as well as tell.'

Statistics confirm her view. In 2019, 75,000 people visited Bolney – and they bought almost a quarter of the estate's production. Move on a few years, and perhaps that quarter will seem insignificant. Sam Linter would like more than half of Bolney's bottles to be sold direct, to visitors and via the website.

English wine tourism in Sussex and beyond goes much further than having a shop filled with bottles and inviting visitors to see the vines growing, understand how the wine is

Stay at Tinwood, overlooking the vines.

made and taste it on the spot. While all that wins converts, who continue to buy the wine and persuade their friends to do the same, plenty of Sussex estates are keen to entice visitors to stay longer.

Do more than visit, stay on the vineyard

At Tinwood Estate, a Ridgeview partner to the north east of Chichester, three luxury lodges – happily named 'Chardonnay', 'Pinot Noir' and 'Pinot Meunier' – are, as owner Art Tukker emphasises, conveniently close to Goodwood, so fans of motor sport or horse racing can combine their passion with fine wine. At Oxney Organic Estate, on the East Sussex/Kent border, two shepherd's huts overlook the vines and there are three

Chris Foss. Photo by Ian Pack, www.winephotos.uk

converted barns close by. Charles Palmer Winery, also close to Rye, offers atmospheric bed-and-breakfast accommodation in the 16th century National Trust-owned Wickham Manor, again with views of the vines. Most remarkable accommodation of all is at a third estate in the same area: the Hobbit House, with hot tub in the garden, at Oastbrook Estate Vineyard.

At Mannings Heath Golf & Wine Estate near Horsham visitors who rent the 17th century cottage have full access to the clubhouse facilities. And for large – or small – groups, Rathfinny Wine Estate's Flint Barns are set in the heart of the huge vineyard high on the South Downs above Alfriston, and grape-picking can be included at the right time of year.

The marketeers have plenty more ideas: opera or jazz in the vineyard, wine clubs with discounts and special offers, pop-up restaurants, wedding receptions or special birthday parties, food-and-wine-matching experiences, blend-your-own-sparkling-wine sessions, tastings of the components that make up a finished blend, renting a row of vines... Sponsorship of beyond-the-vineyard events gives extra visibility and can open up a wine brand to new consumers.

Bigger, bigger and more exciting

Such enterprise will do a lot to ensure all those coming bottles are poured and enjoyed. What, though, does the future hold for the wines from Sussex and beyond as the years go on?

'The industry will only get bigger and bigger,' says Stephen Skelton, whose long experience and major consultancy role with English vineyards makes him the very best of commentators. And WineGB's Julia Trustram Eve is equally positive: 'We are only at the beginning of what are extremely exciting prospects.'

Much will influence those prospects. Earlier, there was reference to climate change, and that will have major effects. Some predictions are scary – one is that by 2080 it will be too hot to grow white grapes in southern England, so they'll need to be planted in Scotland instead. Another has warned that by 2100 it will no longer be possible for grapes to flourish anywhere in the UK.

Perhaps it's more comfortable not to look that far ahead, and instead anticipate even better ripening for existing vines and perhaps a Sussex future for the likes of sauvignon blanc, chenin blanc, riesling, even reds such as merlot.

Another immediate issue is sustainability, a new favourite word in wine. Organic grape growing can work well in England, as three Sussex vineyards, Davenport, Oxney and Seddlescombe, have been proving for a good many years. More are following them with determined enthusiasm. While even now the English climate makes organic growing a challenge there is absolutely no reason why herbicides, pesticides and other chemical treatments cannot be kept to a minimum.

That is one of the reasons behind the Sustainable Wines of Great Britain scheme, launched publicly by WineGB in spring 2020. The scheme's driving force is Chris Foss, who founded – and headed for 32 years – the Wine Division of Plumpton College and now chairs the committee responsible for drawing up the standards vineyards and wineries need to meet to gain the SWGB certification mark. Ridgeview and Bolney have been represented on the committee from its beginning in January

For a greener wine industry, achieve these aims

Under the SWGB scheme, specific aims are set for producers. For vine growers, the sustainability objectives are to:
- maintain and improve soil health,
- manage vineyard canopies and yields optimally,
- reduce (and optimise) pesticide inputs,
- conserve the vineyard (and surrounding) environment and promote biodiversity,
- reduce vineyard energy input, greenhouse gas emissions and carbon footprint per hectare.

In winemaking, those seeking certification under the scheme need to:
- improve winery design to reduce environmental impact,
- increase energy efficiency,
- reduce the volume of water used per bottle of wine,
- deploy an environmentally responsible waste-water management system,
- reduce the environmental impact of wine packaging,
- reduce the level of greenhouse gas emissions and carbon footprint per bottle of wine.

Chris Foss emphasises the thinking behind the code: 'We have a shared responsibility to minimise our impact on the environment in which we operate and maximise our contribution to environmental sustainability and biodiversity.'

2019, and with four other Sussex vineyards they are among the founder members of the sustainability scheme itself. The first wines to bear the new green logo were still wines from the 2019 vintage.

Overall, says Chris Foss, the aim is to 'develop a wine production industry that is not only economically viable and maintains the highest level of grape and wine quality, but implements vine growing and winemaking practices that are sustainable in the long term'. For producers who can do that there are many benefits, 'including a competitive edge in the marketplace, improved public relations and a reduced impact on the increasingly scarce world resources'.

For some of the detail towards that, over to Graham Linter,

Bolney's Senior Manager IT and a self-confessed recycling evangelist: 'Bolney recycles all of the waste cardboard and glass on-site. We also recycle our farm-use plastic through a specialist farm recycling scheme and all of our pallets are purchased second-hand. We had solar panels fitted to our buildings in 2019 and it's always heartening to see how much green electricity we are producing.'

As well, he targets office colleagues: 'I've got most of them well trained and I regularly take home bags of recycling from the office.' Standard items from those bags go into the family recycling bins; he takes others, from crisp packets to highlighters, to a neighbour for recycling at TerraCycle, raising cash for charities.

Ridgeview has solar panels, too, as part of its sustainability programme. Also, it is one of a tiny number of English wine estates – including, in Sussex, Rathfinny – that have installed innovative Bio-Bubble low-energy winery waste water treatment, hugely reducing the quantity of sludge needing to be removed from the site.

Being sustainable goes beyond greenness. It matters in a business sense, stresses Sam Linter. 'We tend to forget that, especially in times like 2020 when it's really important. It's not

Green surroundings for walkers at Ridgeview.

just important for the survival of the business, it's important for jobs, the economy, you can go further down the line...'

She expresses a frustration felt in many English vineyards that have sustained their businesses over many years, planting small areas at a time because they couldn't afford more vines, needing to source grants and loans to make bigger wineries possible, investing their profits to expand. It's that newcomers can come in with big pots of money and leapfrog over all the slow and steady progress to rapidly become top names.

'That's the nature of the world and I don't blame any of those people at all, it's just mere frustration at that lost opportunity,' she adds. 'We could have done better sooner. We could have made sparkling wine sooner than we did. We could have done more volume, but we didn't. We could have done more with our pinot noir. There were so many opportunities we could have taken but we didn't. We just didn't have the resources.'

Tamara Roberts is resigned at the way big money allows top-level entry into English wine: 'It's inevitable and it happens across the world of wine. Wine attracts that kind of investment, it has a romance to it, and it is a fantastic industry to be involved in, it's growing, it's endless really. And brands are very romantic, aspirational products. You understand why people put their money into it.'

Without loans and grants, companies such as Bolney could not have afforded new buildings.

Will people like those be the future of English wine? Only partly, she argues. Big businesses will take advantage of economies of scale and all that their investment brings, and there will be a comfortable place for small wineries for whom cellar-door sales are most important. The challenge will come for the 'awkward middle', sitting in a kind of no-man's land.

'But I think there will be room for everyone, there always has been and I think there always will be.'

Autumn sunrise at Bolney. Photo by Chris Orange, www.chrisorange.com

Chapter 6

The future, still as well as sparkling

WineGB logo for sparkling wine.

Just as Bolney and Ridgeview have had important roles in the development of wine in Sussex – and in broader England – in their first 50 and 25 years respectively, so they are likely to influence what happens in the future.

Nationally and internationally, there is little doubt that bottle-fermented sparkling wine will attract more attention. It is the 'hero style' for trade association WineGB, which in October 2020 announced the Great British Classic Method campaign, complete with hallmark logo.

'We have long recognised the need to positively differentiate and protect our flagship category – wines produced from the classic method,' explained WineGB chairman Simon Robinson at the launch. 'This campaign has set us on the path to ensure that our classic method wines are more positively recognised among the finest wine regions of the world.'

Ridgeview will be one of the important players in that. Tamara and Simon Roberts are adamant that the estate will continue to look beyond its own business interests to co-operate with other sparkling wine producers. It's telling that

Simon has no concerns, rather the opposite, when awards go to newcomers. Ridgeview was the upstart once, he points out, and the success of today's newcomers proves 'people are taking the industry seriously and people are still creating really good wines'.

'I think it's important the awards are shared around – as long as we get the odd trophy here and there still...' He stresses how a number of the leading sparkling wine producers have grown up together. 'There are close relationships, there is competition but still there is collaboration. We are much stronger together.'

Sam Linter has long 'banged the drum' for more support for still wine alongside sparkling in her roles in the UK wine trade bodies – an effort that saw success in late 2020 when WineGB set up a new committee to discuss just that. Michael Hayward, Bolney winemaker and production manager, firmly supports her, confident that still wines will be much more important in years to come, with pricing that makes them accessible to a wider market.

As Sam looks back, she sees advantages and disadvantages in the five decades of experience at Bolney. 'We've got a lot of knowledge on what does and doesn't work in this country, and we have a lot of background knowledge on what sells.' Being able to build a brand is invaluable, and it takes time for a name to become familiar and the quality of its products respected.

Getting there has been a costly process, however, with what little money that was available not always invested well, with little shared experience to help move forward. Newer competitors have been better funded and have seen how to make that money count.

Will the estate spread in years to come? Probably not, is Sam's expectation. Bolney works closely with neighbouring growers and others in Sussex, with contracts to buy grapes from them, so has fruit from a total vine area of more than 50 hectares. As a result Sam has a range of varieties to work with, from the classic sparkling wine grapes to others better suited to still wine, such as bacchus, pinot gris, rondo and dornfelder.

'We know exactly what works well and I'm happy with the vineyard area we have. Commercially it is probably more sensible to keep a small vineyard and buy from other growers,' she argues. That way, Bolney avoids the cost of maintaining more vines and lessens the risk resulting from a disastrous grape-less year.

Over the coming years, she hopes Bolney will claim more market share, though from a slightly slimmed-down range of wines. 'I really want to make better wines. Red from pinot noir is always going to be the better wine. Pinot noir will become much more exciting in England.'

Ridgeview, with its new winery on stream, is ready to increase its production towards 800,000 bottles a year, and current investment is focused on wine tourism. Location should

Left, a variety too soon: merlot, that won't yet ripen at Bolney; right, varieties no longer grown there: müller thurgau and dunkelfelder (photo by Sarah Cuttle).

encourage that. 'We're 20 minutes from Gatwick, 20 minutes from Brighton, 50 minutes from London,' says Mardi Roberts So there will be more international visitors (like the Japanese who sought out Mardi on a whistle-stop visit to the UK after meeting her on an export trip) alongside the local ones.

Quality matters more and more

Increasingly, England's best wine estates are producing premium bottles. At Ridgeview, this is the Oak Reserve, where new and older French oak barrels used during winemaking and maturation contribute to the wine's rich flavours. But, following the Ridgeview ethos of making fine fizz approachable, it costs £75 rather than the £100-plus asked for plenty of other brands' top cuvées.

Simon Roberts and Oak Reserve. Photo by XDB

Five years ago, Sam Linter would have rejected the idea of going so upmarket. But no longer. A premium sparkling blanc de blancs and a very special pinot noir have been quietly maturing in the cellar, ready to for Bolney's 50th birthday celebrations in 2022.

County-wide, there is an initiative to raise wine quality through the Sussex PDO (protected designation of origin), an effort largely led by Mark Driver, who with his wife Sarah established Rathfinny Wine Estate near Alfriston in 2010. The aim, as stated in the formal application from UK Department for the Environment, Food and Rural Affairs to the European Commission, is 'to ensure that Sussex wines will continue to be considered amongst the very best in the world', reflecting the efforts of the county's winemakers and intending to protect them from unfair competition and consumers from misrepresentation.

At the time of writing, this was waiting for Europe-wide approval but was already in place in the UK as the Sussex Quality Wine Scheme, allowing producers to label their wines Sussex, Sussex Sparkling, Sussex Still or Sussex Origin provided they meet the scheme's rules. These aim to make the designation 'a benchmark denoting high quality still and sparkling wine' and cover such aspects as permitted grape varieties, alcohol level, higher analytical standards, hand harvesting, all grape-growing and winemaking within the county and, for sparkling wines, longer bottle ageing.

There isn't unanimity among Sussex producers on the PDO. Doubters argue that the UK industry is too young to split its message through regional labelling – there's time for that once English wine as a whole has a much higher profile both at home and abroad – and that Sussex is an administrative area rather than a specific geographical region. But there is wide agreement that aspirations to set the bar higher for the quality of English wine should be welcomed.

Those who make wine in Sussex aren't alone in wanting to create a higher-quality product. Consumers increasingly demand information on the origin and means of production of the bottles they buy, and while they may be drinking less they are ready to pay more for wine they'll enjoy. More of them are drinking English wine, and often they aren't the same people who supported English vineyards in the past.

'When we started it was very much a demographic of middle age, middle class,' says Simon Roberts. 'Now it's very much wider.'

In marketing speak, customers at both Ridgeview and Bolney fall into two categories, the 'adventurous connoisseurs' and the 'generation treaters'. The former are generally older, wine-experienced people. 'They will always be there and are a great market for us,' says Sam Linter. The latter group are younger – the millennials – and present an interesting challenge. 'They have a very different outlook on wine than we had at their age,' she continues. 'They're a very well informed market.'

Both she and Simon highlight the green enthusiasm of younger buyers: they have environmental concerns – on food miles, local provenance – and they want to see where the wine

A very different demographic: visitors in Bolney's café.

Café terrace with view over the vines at Bolney. Photo by Chris Orange, www.chrisorange.com

they buy comes from. They also bring their children when they visit, something that simply didn't happen a decade ago.

'We make more of the type of wines they are enjoying,' Sam continues, instancing the bubbles – rosé especially – and still wines from grapes whose names are memorable and easy to pronounce, grapes that are seen in bottles from other countries. The new Bolney chardonnay is largely a result of such consumer demand. And, of course, there are bubbles galore at Ridgeview.

Mardi Roberts echoes Sam's point on consumer knowledge: 'People are no longer surprised by English sparkling wine, now people have their favourite house. It has been a very remarkable revolution.'

All this is about the present and near future. Let's look much further ahead. How will Ridgeview and Bolney be remembered when they have doubled their present life-spans?

Chris Roberts believes that in 25 years time Ridgeview will be recognised for 'crashing the barrier'. Son Simon continues: 'Mum and Dad will very much be regarded as pioneers. We and Nyetimber really started to put the English wine industry on the map internationally. We will be seen as guiding the industry to where it is now, the professionalism, the export side of things, the international aspiration, how the public perceive English wine.'

But there will be no resting on laurels. 'There are always new things to do, so much depends on what people want.' insists Chris. 'We have just got to aim to be the best.'

'Pioneer' is also a word Sam Linter uses for her 50-year heritage. 'I would really like to think Bolney was regarded as one of the pioneers, a family business that took a gamble on starting something that people said couldn't be done. And

took a gamble on red wine, pinot noir particularly, when again people said it couldn't be done.'

She goes further: 'I would like Bolney to be remembered as a producer who made really, really good wines but at the same time wanted to be very approachable. We have never wanted to be uber-luxury or exclusive.'

Like Chris Roberts, she acknowledges that the job is never done. 'One thing I have learned in 25 years: you can't stop here.' Predicting where the business will be in the future isn't possible, 'because in two years, in five years, it changes'. 'You have to adapt, it is changing all the time.'

Finally, let's stop being so serious and allow Mardi Roberts to add one extra, essential aspect: 'We have made wine fun and we will continue to do so.'

And how better to end this book than with the words of Tamara Roberts' husband Lardy, who likens Ridgeview to a flag bearer – and I'm sure he's happy to let Bolney share in the carrying. 'You always need someone to run in front – but not warning people with a red flag, instead telling them about something exciting.' In 25 years time, in 50 years time that something exciting, he predicts, 'will still be on everyone's lips'.

Lardy, ready to run in front with exciting bottles rather than a red flag.

Pioneers: the family trees

Rodney & Janet (d. 2006) **Pratt**

Mike (d. 2014) *& Chris Roberts*

Sam & Graham Linter

Tamara Roberts &
Simon (Lardy) Larder

Simon & Mardi Roberts

Charlotte
Linter

THE
BOLNEY
SUSSEX *Estate* ENGLAND

RIDGEVIEW
ENGLAND

Acknowledgements

Many people have helped in the production of this book, sharing information and providing illustrations, showing me around vineyards and wineries, answering questions, reading and commenting on the text at various stages and generally doing much to help me achieve what you now read. I am grateful to them all, and if there are errors, they are mine, not theirs.

Particular thanks are due to Alison Barclay and to my husband, Jean Sagues, for their patient involvement and continuing support. I appreciate, too, the help of Chris Foss, Sue Olford, Ian Pack, Avril Sargent, Kristin Syltevik and Anne Wilson, as well as that of Robin Tyler and Jon Bull at Selsey Press. The late Lena Inger, whose inspiration encouraged my wine writing career, urged me long ago write a book about wine people. Finally, this is it.

A number of illustrations have been sourced through Wikimedia Commons; these are images existing in the public domain or made available under Creative Commons attribution-only licence CC BY 4.0 (https://creativecommons.org/licenses/by-sa/4.0/). Specifically, these are King John (page 12), Sir Kenelm Digby (page 17), Barbe-Nicole Ponsardin and Louise Pommery (page 26), vine mildew (page 50), phylloxera bug model (page 52, photographer: Rodney Start, Museums Victoria, https://collections.museumsvictoria.com.au/specimens/2301941) and spotted wing drosophilia (page 55, Shane F. McEvey, Australian Museum). The image of Samuel Pepys (page 12) is from the Wellcome Collection under the same Creative Commons licence.

Images from external sources are copyright protected and are not to be reproduced in any form without prior written permission from the copyright source. Every effort has been made to trace rights holders, but if any have been inadvertently overlooked please contact the author/publisher.

Index

To include all references to Bolney and Ridgeview, and to the principal family members of the two estate (Mike, Chris, Tamara & Simon Roberts, and Rodney & Janet Pratt & Sam Linter), would totally overwhelm this index, so they are excluded – as are references to the most common grapes used in sparkling wine making, chardonnay, pinot meunier and pinot noir.

A

acidity 23, 24, 43, 59,64, 67, 69, 72
Albourne Estate 6, 29, 48, 66, 80
alcohol 23, 51, 57, 59, 63, 67, 90
Australia 36, 46

B

barrels 22, 43, 44, 56, 62, 89
base wine 44, 46, 49, 64, 66, 67
Bio-Bubble 84
blanc de blancs 12, 70, 74, 76, 89
blending 44, 66, 70, 82
Bollinger, Lily 26
botrytis 45, 50, 61, 63
bottle-fermented 10, 16, 18, 87
bottling 41, 43, 44, 46, 49, 65, 66

Breaky Bottom 48
Brock, Raymond Barrington 13, 16

C
canes 42, 44, 45
canopy management 24, 49, 52, 55, 57, 67
Carr Taylor, David & Linda 16
chalk 7
Chapel Down 14
champagne 7, 12, 14, 16, 17, 21, 26-27, 28,
        47, 48, 76, 77, 78
chaptalisation 64
Charles Palmer Winery 82
chemicals 45, 50, 83
Clarke, Oz 12, 24
climate change 7, 24, 38, 52, 60, 82, 83
Cliquot, la Veuve 26-27
contract winemaking 19, 70-72
corks 46, 53, 55, 66, 68, 70
Covid-19 77-78
crop size 47, 56, 57, 58

D
Davenport Vineyards 83
Denbies Wine Estate 59
Devon 60
Digby, Sir Kenelm 17
disgorgement 26, 53, 54, 55
Domesday Book 11, 15
dosage 26, 55
Downs, South & North 4, 7, 30, 48, 82
Driver, Mark 89

E
English Wine Producers 39
English Wine Week 51, 79
European Commission 68, 89
European Union 25
Essex 8, 57, 63
export 27, 51, 76-77, 89, 92

F
Family Business United 39
fermentation 16, 17, 20, 26, 47, 49, 50, 51,
53, 57, 61, 63-64, 65, 66, 67-68
        malolactic 64
fining 43, 60
floral initiation 52
flowering 47, 51-52, 55-56, 75
food pairing 73-74, 80, 82
Foss, Chris 82, 83-84
Fourie, Johann 31, 80
frost prevention 42, 47-48, 49

G
gin 66
Goring, Pip 30
Great British Classic Method 87
grape varieties
        bacchus 30, 48, 58, 88
        dornfelder 20, 21, 48, 66, 73, 74, 88
        hybrid 48
        müller-thurgau 19, 23, 88
        ortega 48
        pinot blanc 48

        pinot gris 48, 74, 88
        pinotage 30
        reichensteiner 16
        regent 48
        rondo 20, 21, 48, 66, 73, 88
        sauvignon blanc 24, 48, 83
        seyval blanc 48
        solaris 48
Greatrix, Brad 31, 80
greensand 7, 16
gyropalettes 53, 54

H
Hall, Peter 48
Hampshire 8, 11, 12, 13, 52, 63
harvesting 12, 23, 30, 57-63, 71, 72, 90
        green 57 mechanical 59
Hayward, Mike 43, 69-70, 72, 74, 87
Heerema, Eric 31
Henriot, Apolline 26-27

I / J / K / L
International Wine & Spirit Competition
        (IWSC) 19, 38, 39
Jacquinot, Jean-Manuel 16, 17
King John 12
Kent 8, 47, 61, 63, 81
Larder, Simon ('Lardy') 35-36, 92, 93
Laurent-Perrier, Mathilde Emilie 26
lees 26, 50-51, 65, 68
Leonardslee Gardens 30, 31

Lindlar, Kit 16, 17, 19, 22

M / N / O
Mannings Heath Estate 6, 30, 76, 80, 82
Merret, Christopher 17
mildew 23, 45, 50
Moss, Stuart & Sandy 15-16
Nightingale, Alison 30
Nutbourne Vineyards 6, 48, 79
Nyetimber Estate 6, 8, 12, 15-16, 18, 31, 52, 61, 80, 91
Oastbrook Estate Vineyard 80
oidium 50
Olry-Roederer, Camille 26, 27
organic growing 30, 45, 60, 63, 81, 83
Oxney Organic Estate 6, 30, 45, 60, 81, 83

P
pandemic 72, 77, 80
Pepys, Samuel 12
Pérignon, Dom 17
pesticides 83
pests 46, 53
    moths 53
    phylloxera 52, 53
    spotted wing drosophila 55
Plumpton College 6, 8, 9, 16, 17, 19, 22, 29, 59, 67, 69, 83
Pommery, Louise 26
Pratt, Mark 18, 35
pressing 12, 58, 59, 61, 62, 63
pruning 41, 42, 44, 64, 66, 67

R
racking 43, 64, 65, 66
Rathfinny Wine Estate 6, 80, 82, 84, 89
recently disgorged (RD) 26
recycling 50, 84
Ridgefest 79, 81
ripeness 7, 8, 24, 42, 48, 57, 58-59, 72, 83, 88
Roberts, Mardi 36-37, 74, 76-77, 80, 89, 91, 92, 93
Romans 11

S
Salisbury-Jones, Sir Guy 13
Scotland 83
screw caps 46
second fermentation 16, 17, 27, 49, 50, 51, 53, 67, 68
Seddlescombe Organic Vineyard 83
Skelton, Stephen 82
South East Vineyards Association 39
sparging 43
spraying 45, 50, 61
Spriggs, Cherie 31, 80
stabilisation 43
Stopham Estate 6, 25, 48
Streeter, Penny 30, 31
Strugnell, Matt 42, 49, 52, 56, 58, 60, 63, 64, 74
sulphur 43, 45, 60
Sussex Business Awards 38
Sussex Business Women Excellence Awards 39
Sussex Modern 80

Sussex PDO 68, 89-90
Sussex Quality Wine Scheme 89
sustainability 38, 45, 64, 83
Sustainable Wine GB 83-84
sweet wines 48, 58, 61, 63
Syltevik, Kristin 30, 45, 60

T
tannin 58, 66, 68
tartaric acid 43
TCA 46
Tinwood 6, 81
tirage 46, 67
trellis 43, 45, 49, 64
Trustram Eve, Julia 24, 82

U / V
UK Vineyards Association 39
veraison 57
vermouth 66
Vine-Works 43, 49, 61, 64
vintage 19, 37, 43, 46, 72, 75, 84
vintage wines 12, 16, 21, 27, 30, 44, 50, 51, 70, 76

W / Y
Waitrose 21
WineGB 8, 24, 39, 56, 77, 82, 83, 87
WineGB Awards 39
Wine tourism 9, 30, 51, 81
Wiston Estate 6, 30
yeast 27, 46, 50, 51, 53, 57, 63, 65, 67